YOUR TAX FO
MADE EASY

1999

GRAHAM M. KITCHEN FCA

CONSULTANT EDITOR
BRIAN GILLIGAN FCA, ATII, TEP
OF BDO STOY HAYWARD,
CHARTERED ACCOUNTANTS

foulsham
LONDON • NEW YORK • TORONTO • SYDNEY

foulsham

The Publishing House, Bennetts Close
Cippenham, Slough, Berks SL1 5AP

ISBN 0-572-02502-5

Printed in Great Britain by Redwood Books Ltd., Trowbridge.

Contents

Introduction

How to use this book

When you get a tax form, look it up in the contents page of this book to identify it, turn to the appropriate chapter and it will tell you about the form. If you have to fill it in, then it will tell you what to fill in and where to get the information – plus a few tax tips along the way! There is a summary of rates and allowances, including those announced in the March 1999 Budget, on page 72.

Tax return form

Not everyone gets a tax return automatically. They are normally sent out to people who have more than one source of income; to all company directors; to the self-employed and to anyone whose tax affairs are fairly complex.

The fact that you do not get a tax return doesn't mean that you don't have to send one in.

The responsibility is yours – not your employer's, nor the tax office's. If you have received earnings or income which hasn't been taxed, or you think you have paid too much tax and you are entitled to a tax refund, then you should fill in a tax return.

You have the opportunity to work out, on tax calculation forms, your own tax liability or tax refund if you so wish. (see page 64).

Where do you get a form?

If you want a tax return form or one of the supplementary pages, telephone the special Inland Revenue order line on 0645 000404 or fax 0645 000604. You will need to quote your name, address and NI reference number. The Inland Revenue have a Helpline which you can ring on 0645 000444. A Braille version of the self assessment guide is also available on 01274 539646.

When should you fill in a tax return?

Unfortunately, the tax year does not follow the calendar year – it runs from 6 April to 5 April – just to confuse everyone!

The 1999 tax return covers your income, capital gains, reliefs and allowances for the year ended 5 April 1999.

Although it is called a self assessment tax return you do not have to calculate your own tax if you don't want to. Provided that you send in your tax return by 30 September 1999 the tax office will do it for you.

If you wish to use the tax calculator working sheets provided with your tax return, then you have until 31 January 2000 to send in your return (see page 64).

Payments on account

If you have not paid most of your tax by deduction, or you are self-employed, you should have paid an amount on account of your 1998–99 tax liability on 31 January 1999. (see page 29).

Don't be late

There will be an automatic penalty of £100 if your tax return is not sent in by 31 January 2000 and another £100 six months later if it is still overdue. (These are reduced if the tax due is less than £100.)

There will be further penalties if you continue to be late. In addition, interest and surcharges will be charged on overdue tax.

Do you have to fill in a tax return if you are *always* due a refund?

No, the tax office will probably send you a Form R40 which is a simplified form of return and which should result in your tax refund coming through regularly and quickly (see page 56).

Go back six years

If you find you have been paying too much tax this year, there is a good chance that this has happened in previous years. You can go back six years to reclaim tax.

Are you claiming tax refunds due to you?

The Inland Revenue estimates that around seven million pensioners, married women and children are not claiming their tax refunds.

If your total income does not exceed your tax allowances and you have received any income from which tax has been deducted, you should claim it back. Turn to page 56 for advice on what to do.

If you are on PAYE

Don't assume that your PAYE code is correct. Your employer cannot check it for you – you must do it yourself (see page 52); it's also up to you to check that the tax that you have paid during the year is correct (see page 58).

What to do if you don't get a reply from your tax office

Under the Taxpayer's Charter you should not have to wait more than eight weeks for a query to be dealt with. Contact your local tax enquiry office if you have a query, then your tax inspector.

If you still do not get satisfaction, write to the District Inspector and as a last resort the Regional Controller (or your MP) – all telephone numbers are in the telephone directory under Inland Revenue.

How this book can help you

Each page corresponds to a section of your tax return or tax form, and you are told what to enter, what not to enter and where to find the information that the tax office needs.

There are many tax tips and additional chapters to give you extra advice in claiming tax back and checking your own tax.

Why this book is useful to you

1. it will make it easier for you to fill in your tax return;
2. it will tell you whether you are due a tax refund and, more importantly, how to claim it;
3. you will avoid paying too much tax because you can identify the form you have received and know what to do with it;
4. you can fill in the tax return form reproduced in this book so that you have a permanent copy to which you may refer at any time.

How to fill in your tax return

Start filling in your new self assessment tax return by ticking either the 'No' or 'Yes' boxes (Q1 to Q9) on page 2 of the return (reproduced below).

If you tick 'Yes' in any box, check to see if the tax office have sent you the supplementary pages to complete and tick them off in the right hand column.

You will need supplementary pages if you are:

Code sequence		Page in this book
1	In employment	31
2	Participating in share schemes	35
3	Self-employed	36
4	In partnership	42
5	Owning land or property	44
6	Receiving foreign income	47
7	Receiving income from trusts or estates	48
8	Declaring capital gains or losses	49
9	Non-resident in the U.K.	51

If you need supplementary pages and you have not been sent them with your tax return, ring the Inland Revenue order line on 0645 000404 (fax 0645 000604) and ask for the missing pages.
You will need to quote your name, address and NI reference number.

Inland Revenue

INCOME AND CAPITAL GAINS *for the year ended 5 April 1999*

Step 1 Answer Questions 1 to 9 below to find out if you have the right supplementary Pages. Please read pages 6 and 7 of your Tax Return Guide if you need help. The Questions are colour coded to help you identify the supplementary Pages and their guidance notes. If you answer 'No', go to the next question. If you answer 'Yes', you must complete the relevant supplementary Pages. Turn to the back of your Tax Return to see if you have the right ones and look at the back of the Tax Return Guide to see if you have guidance notes to go with them. **Ring the Orderline on 0645 000 404, or fax on 0645 000 604 for any you need (open 7 days a week between 8am and 10pm). If I have sent you any Pages you do not need, ignore them.**

Check to make sure you have the right supplementary Pages and then tick the box below.

Q1 Were you an employee, or office holder, or director, or agency worker or did you receive payments or benefits from a former employer (excluding a pension) in the year ended 5 April 1999? NO ☐ YES ☐ — EMPLOYMENT YES ☐

Q2 Did you have any taxable income from share options, shares (but this does not include dividends - they go in Question 10) or share related benefits in the year? NO ☐ YES ☐ — SHARE SCHEMES YES ☐

Q3 Were you self-employed (but not in partnership)? (Tick 'Yes' if you were a Name at Lloyd's) NO ☐ YES ☐ — SELF-EMPLOYMENT YES ☐

Q4 Were you in partnership? NO ☐ YES ☐ — PARTNERSHIP YES ☐

Q 5 Did you receive any rent or other income from land and property in the UK?

NO ☐ YES ☐   **LAND & PROPERTY YES** ☐

Q 6 Did you have any taxable income from overseas pensions or benefits, or from foreign companies or savings institutions, offshore funds or trusts abroad, or from land and property abroad or gains on foreign insurance policies?

NO ☐ YES ☐

Have you or could you have received, or enjoyed directly or indirectly, or benefited in any way from, income of a foreign entity as a result of a transfer of assets made in this or earlier years?

NO ☐ YES ☐

Do you want to claim tax credit relief for foreign tax paid on foreign income or gains?

NO ☐ YES ☐   **FOREIGN YES** ☐

Q 7 Did you receive, or are you deemed to have, income from a trust, settlement or deceased person's estate?

NO ☐ YES ☐   **TRUSTS ETC YES** ☐

Q 8 Capital gains
- Have you disposed of your exempt only or main residence? If 'Yes', read page 7 of your Tax Return Guide to see if you need the Capital Gains Pages.

NO ☐ YES ☐

- Did you dispose of other chargeable assets worth more than £13,600 in total?

NO ☐ YES ☐

- Were your total chargeable gains more than £6,800?

NO ☐ YES ☐   **CAPITAL GAINS YES** ☐

You must also fill in the Capital Gains Pages if you wish to claim a capital loss.

Q 9 Are you claiming that you were not resident, or not ordinarily resident, or not domiciled, in the UK, or dual resident in the UK and another country, for all or part of the year?

NO ☐ YES ☐   **NON-RESIDENCE ETC YES** ☐

Step 2 **Please use blue or black ink to fill in your Tax Return and please do not include pence.** Round down, to the nearest pound, your income and capital gains and round up your tax credits and tax deductions.
Now fill in any supplementary Pages BEFORE going to Step 3.

Tick this box when you have filled in your supplementary Pages ☐

Step 3 Now fill in Questions 10 to 23. If you answer 'No' to a question, go to the next one. If you answer 'Yes', fill in the relevant boxes.

Remember
- You do not have to calculate your tax - I will do it for you if you send your Tax Return to me by 30 September. This will save you time and effort.
- The Tax Calculation Guide I have sent you will help if you decide to calculate the tax yourself.
- You do not have to wait until 30 September 1999, or 31 January 2000, to send me your Tax Return.

The next step

If you have ticked any of the 'Yes' boxes above then the next step is to fill in those supplementary pages – turn to the appropriate page reference in this book before you go on to complete the rest of the tax return.

If you have ticked all the 'No' boxes, then start to fill in page 3 of your tax return which covers income from UK savings and investments.

The tax return is reproduced on the following pages.

There is a 'Fill this in if …' box after each section so that you can identify quickly whether it applies to you or not. If it does, there are boxes telling you where to find the information, what to enter and some tax tips along the way.

Q10 Income from U.K. savings and investments

If you receive income from U.K. savings and investments tick the 'Yes' box and fill in the information requested. If you tick the 'No' box turn to Q11 on page 12.

INCOME *for the year ended 5 April 1999*

Q 10 **Did you receive any income from UK savings and investments?** **NO** [ ] **YES** [ ]

If yes, fill in boxes 10.1 to 10.32 as appropriate. Include only your share from any joint savings and investments.

■ *Interest*

● Interest from UK banks, building societies and deposit takers

	Taxable amount
- where **no tax** has been deducted	**10.1** £

	Amount after tax deducted	Tax deducted	Gross amount before tax
- where **tax has** been deducted	**10.2** £	**10.3** £	**10.4** £

FILL THIS IN IF:

You have savings accounts with banks, building societies and other deposit takers in the U.K.

WHERE TO FIND THE INFORMATION

Your bank, building society, etc. should send you an annual statement showing the interest earned and any tax deducted. If you do not receive a statement, ask for one.

What to enter

You do not need to state the name of the bank, building society, etc.

Where no tax has been deducted, fill in box 10.1 with the *total* amount you received in the year ended 5 April 1999.

Where tax *has* been deducted, fill in boxes 10.2, 10.3 and 10.4 with the totals .

You will need to keep a note of how you arrive at the total – use the tax organiser on page 73 of this book.

TAX TIP:

If you have savings or investments held in joint names, the interest is normally divided equally when filling in tax returns. If the ownership is not held equally, then you should ask the tax office for form 17 in which you can jointly declare the actual ownership split. You then enter the amounts accordingly in your tax returns. Such declaration takes effect from the date it is made, provided that the form is sent to the tax office within 60 days.

TAX TIP:

Did you receive your interest gross, or net of tax?
If you did not instruct your bank or building society to pay your interest gross by filling in form R85, then they will deduct tax. If your total earnings and income in 1999-2000 is likely to be less than £4,335 you should ask your bank or building society for form R85 otherwise you will have to reclaim the tax at the end of the year (see page 56).

- Interest distributions from UK authorised unit trusts and open-ended investment companies (dividend distributions go below)

Amount after tax deducted	Tax deducted	Gross amount before tax
10.5 £	**10.6** £	**10.7** £

What to enter

The total gross amount, total tax deducted and total after tax.

If you received interest without tax being deducted, include the figure in 10.7, with a zero value in your total for box 10.6.

Do not include any 'equalisation' receipts.

FILL THIS IN IF:

You have interest from U.K. unit trusts, etc.

WHERE TO FIND THE INFORMATION

Your unit trust, etc. will provide you with a tax voucher.

- National Savings (other than FIRST Option Bonds and the first £70 of interest from a National Savings Ordinary Account)

	Taxable amount
	10.8 £

- National Savings FIRST Option Bonds

Amount after tax deducted	Tax deducted	Gross amount before tax
10.9 £	**10.10** £	**10.11** £

What to enter

The total interest received or credited in your accounts in the year ended 5 April 1999 in respect of the National Savings accounts and Bonds listed goes in box 10.8. Interest from FIRST Option Bonds will have had tax deducted so fill in the boxes 10.9, 10.10 and 10.11 for these.

FILL THIS IN IF:

You have any National Savings ordinary or investment accounts, deposit, income or capital bonds, Pensioners Guaranteed Income Bonds or FIRST Option Bonds.

DO NOT FILL THIS IN IF:

You only have interest from any National Savings Certificates, or Children's Bonus Bonds – these do not have to be declared in your tax return. Neither do you need to give details of any Premium Bond prizes.

WHERE TO FIND THE INFORMATION

If you receive interest from a National Savings ordinary account, send your book to National Savings, Glasgow, G58 1SB to have the interest added. Show the total interest in your tax return but exclude the first £70 of interest as it is tax free. Interest is credited automatically on your Investment account every 31 December and a statement will be sent to you if you request one. The tax office will accept this December interest figure as the figure to go in your tax return, you do not have to apportion it on a time basis. National Savings will send you an annual statement of interest earned on Bonds in April each year.

	Amount after tax deducted	Tax deducted	Gross amount before tax
• Other income from UK savings and investments (except dividends)	**10.12** £	**10.13** £	**10.14** £

FILL THIS IN IF:

You have any income from U.K. savings, etc. not covered in the earlier sections. These could include, for example, purchased annuities (but not those arising from a personal pension or retirement contract); income from Government stocks; friendly societies. This section could also be used for profits on relevant discounted securities and profits on selling certificates of deposit, etc.

WHERE TO FIND THE INFORMATION

Annuity statements and other documentation, certificates and interest vouchers from investment and insurance companies.

TAX TIP:

If most of your income comes from interest and dividends, you are probably due a tax refund – see page 56.

What to enter

The total amount received, tax credit or tax deducted and gross income.

If you have accrued income reliefs exceeding charges, the net figure should be deducted from box 10.14 without any adjustment to box 10.13. (see also page 15).

Do not include any dividends – this section is for interest only.

■ *Dividends*

	Dividend/distribution	Tax credit	Dividend/distribution plus credit
• Dividends and other qualifying distributions from UK companies	**10.15** £	**10.16** £	**10.17** £

	Dividend/distribution	Tax credit	Dividend/distribution plus credit
• Dividend distributions from UK authorised unit trusts and open-ended investment companies	**10.18** £	**10.19** £	**10.20** £

	Dividend	Notional tax	Dividend plus notional tax
• Scrip dividends from UK companies	**10.21** £	**10.22** £	**10.23** £

	Dividend	Notional tax	Dividend plus notional tax
• Foreign income dividends from UK companies	**10.24** £	**10.25** £	**10.26** £

	Dividend	Notional tax	Dividend plus notional tax
• Foreign income dividend distributions from UK authorised unit trusts and open-ended investment companies	**10.27** £	**10.28** £	**10.29** £

	Notional tax	Taxable amount
• Non-qualifying distributions and loans written off	**10.30** £	**10.31** £	**10.32** £

FILL THIS IN IF:

You received dividends or foreign income dividends from U.K. companies.

WHERE TO FIND THE INFORMATION

The dividend vouchers and distribution receipts will show all these details and will also state whether the dividend is classed as a foreign income dividend.

What to enter

Put in each of the boxes the total amounts you received, the tax credit (or notional income tax) and the gross amount (the dividend received plus the tax credit).Include scrip and stock dividends but do not include 'equalisation' receipts.

Q11   Income from U.K. pensions and social security benefits

If you received income from a U.K. pension, retirement annuity or Social Security benefit tick the 'Yes' box and fill in the information requested. If you tick the 'No' box turn to Q12 on page 14.

INCOME *for the year ended 5 April 1999, continued*

Q11   **Did you receive a UK pension, retirement annuity or Social Security benefit?**   **NO** ☐   **YES** ☐   If yes, fill in boxes 11.1 to 11.13 as appropriate.

■   *State pensions and benefits*   Taxable amount for 1998-99

●   State Retirement Pension   **11.1** £

●   Widow's Pension   **11.2** £

●   Widowed Mother's Allowance   **11.3** £

FILL THIS IN IF:

You were entitled to a State pension or widow's pension between 6 April 1998 and 5 April 1999 or widowed mother's allowance.

WHERE TO FIND THE INFORMATION

You should have a statement from the Department of Social Security of the pensions and allowances to which you are entitled – if not, ask at your local office.

What to enter

Any basic state pension including any earnings-related pension, graduated pension and age addition. A married man should only enter amounts payable to him; a married woman should enter amounts payable to her in *her* tax return (even if paid as a result of her husband's contributions), including any widow's pension or widowed mother's allowance.

Do not enter

The state Christmas bonus or other social security benefits in this section.

TAX TIP:

If the State pension is going to be your only income, then you can, and should, apply to your local Social Security Office for income support, housing benefit and various other social security benefits which are not taxable and need not be included in your tax return. Also apply to your local council for a reduction in your council tax.

• Industrial Death Benefit Pension		**11.4** £
• Jobseeker's Allowance		**11.5** £
• Invalid Care Allowance		**11.6** £
• Statutory Sick Pay and Statutory Maternity Pay paid by the Department of Social Security		**11.7** £

	Tax deducted	Gross amount before tax
• Taxable Incapacity Benefit	**11.8** £	**11.9** £

FILL THIS IN IF:

You received or were entitled to any of the following benefits in the year ended 5 April 1999. Industrial death benefit, statutory sick pay and maternity pay paid by DSS, jobseeker's allowance, incapacity benefit, invalid care allowance.

WHERE TO FIND THE INFORMATION

Your benefit office will have given you a statement or form showing the amount payable and, where applicable, the taxable portion of the benefit.

TAX TIP:

If you receive a pension in addition to the State pension it is possible you may be able to claim some tax back (see page 56).

What to enter

State the taxable amount received or due to you for the year ended 5 April 1999 in the relevant box.

In the case of Incapacity Benefit the DSS will give you a form advising of the tax position. (It is not taxable for the first 28 weeks of incapacity or if paid when incapacity began before 13 April 1995 and for which invalidity benefit used to be payable.)

Statutory Sick Pay or Statutory Maternity Pay should only be shown if paid direct to you by the DSS; if it was paid to you by your employer then it will be included on your P60 or P45 form.

■ Other pensions and retirement annuities

	Amount after tax deducted	Tax deducted	Gross amount before tax
• Pensions (other than State pensions) and retirement annuities	**11.10** £	**11.11** £	**11.12** £

	Amount of deduction	
• Deduction - see the note for box 11.13 on page 14 of your Tax Return Guide	**11.13** £	

FILL THIS IN IF:

You received a pension other than the State pension between 6 April 1998 and 5 April 1999.

WHERE TO FIND THE INFORMATION

At the end of each tax year the company paying you the pension must send you a P60 form (see page 58) or a statement by 31 May 1999.

What to enter

The gross amount received, the tax deducted and the amount actually received in the year ended 5 April 1999.

Certain pensions are exempted in whole or part from U.K. tax, in which case enter the amount in box 11.13.

Q12 Other income you may have received

If you received income from taxable maintenance or alimony, gains on U.K. life insurance policies, or refunds of surplus additional voluntary pension contributions tick the 'Yes' box and fill in the information requested. If you tick the 'No' box move on to Q13 below.

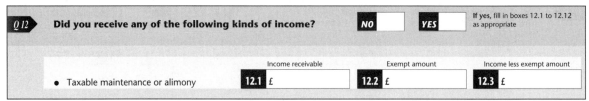

Q 12	**Did you receive any of the following kinds of income?**		NO	YES	If yes, fill in boxes 12.1 to 12.12 as appropriate

		Income receivable	Exempt amount	Income less exempt amount
●	Taxable maintenance or alimony	**12.1** £	**12.2** £	**12.3** £

FILL THIS IN IF:

You received maintenance or alimony under a court order or agreement for the maintenance of yourself or your children.

Do not enter voluntary payments.

WHERE TO FIND THE INFORMATION

The court order, legal agreement or Child Support Agency assessment will show the amount due.

What to enter

Show the amount received in year ended 5 April 1999 in box 12.1.

Enter the exempted amount (up to £1,900) in box 12.2.

The amount paid will be exempted up to this figure if the payments are from your separated or divorced husband or wife and they are for yourself or to support a child and you have not remarried or reverted to living again with your husband or wife from whom you were previously separated.

		Number of years		Amount of gain(s)
●	Gains on UK life insurance policies etc (without notional tax)	**12.4**		**12.5** £

		Number of years	Notional tax	Amount of gain(s)
●	Gains on UK life insurance policies etc (with notional tax) - read page 15 of the Tax Return Guide	**12.6**	**12.7** £	**12.8** £

		Amount	
●	Corresponding deficiency relief	**12.9** £	

		Amount received	Notional tax	Amount plus notional tax
●	Refunds of surplus funds from additional voluntary contributions	**12.10** £	**12.11** £	**12.12** £

FILL THIS IN IF:

You made gains on U.K. life insurance policies or you received a repayment from a FSAVC pension scheme.

WHERE TO FIND THE INFORMATION

The insurance company or Scheme's Trustees will have given you a statement containing the figures.

What to enter

In the case of life policies, the relevant number of years, notional tax and amounts received as shown on the insurance company's statement; for AVC refunds, the amounts received and notional tax figures.

Q13 Miscellaneous income

If you received any other income not covered in your tax return, then tick the 'Yes' box. Such income could include casual work, insurance or mail order commission, royalties, accrued income charges, post-cessation receipts, etc. If you tick 'No' then move on to Q14.

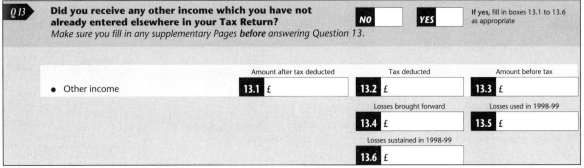

		Amount after tax deducted	Tax deducted	Amount before tax
• Other income		**13.1** £	**13.2** £	**13.3** £
			Losses brought forward	Losses used in 1998-99
			13.4 £	**13.5** £
			Losses sustained in 1998-99	
			13.6 £	

Q 13 **Did you receive any other income which you have not already entered elsewhere in your Tax Return?** *Make sure you fill in any supplementary Pages before answering Question 13.* NO ☐ YES ☐ If yes, fill in boxes 13.1 to 13.6 as appropriate

FILL THIS IN IF:

You received any miscellaneous income not declared anywhere else in your tax return including accrued income charges.

WHERE TO FIND THE INFORMATION

Statements, receipts, invoices, contract notes, etc.

TAX TIP:

If you prefer, you can have post-cessation receipts taxed in the year in which the business ceased, in which case don't complete this section but tick box 22.5 (see page 27).

What to enter

The amount received in the year ended 5 April 1999 after claiming any allowable expenses (see page 34).

If tax has been deducted this must be shown. If you have losses brought forward, or you are creating a loss in this year, then these amounts must also be shown.

Include in box 13.3 accrued income charges if they exceed any accrued income reliefs.

Q14 Relief for pension contributions

If you are a member of your employer's pension scheme and no other scheme and all your contributions have been deducted at source, then tick the 'No' box and move to Q15. (You will get tax relief on these contributions deducted from your pay.) Tick the 'Yes' box if you want to claim relief for other pension scheme contributions

Maximum contributions allowable for tax as a percentage of your earnings (see page 16)

Age at beginning of tax year	Retirement annuity premium %	Personal pension plan %
up to 35	17.5	17.5
36 to 45	17.5	20
46 to 50	17.5	25
51 to 55	20	30
56 to 60	22.5	35
61 to 74	27.5	40

For plans taken out after 14 March 1989 the maximum net relevant earnings figures on which relief is available are as follows:

From 6 April:			
1991	£71,400	1995	£78,600
1992	£75,000	1996	£82,200
1993	£75,000	1997	£84,000
1994	£76,800	1998	£87,600

The figure from 6 April 1999 will be £90,600.

RELIEFS *for the year ended 5 April 1999*

Q14 **Do you want to claim relief for pension contributions?**   NO ☐   YES ☐   If yes, fill in boxes 14.1 to 14.17 as appropriate.

*Do not include contributions deducted from your pay by your employer to their pension scheme, because tax relief is given automatically. But **do include** your contributions to personal pension schemes.*

- **Retirement annuity contracts**

Qualifying payments made in 1998-99	**14.1** £	1998-99 payments used in an earlier year	**14.2** £	**Relief claimed**
1998-99 payments now to be carried back	**14.3** £	Payments brought back from 1999-2000	**14.4** £	box 14.1 *minus* (boxes 14.2 and 14.3, but not 14.4) **14.5** £

- **Self-employed contributions to personal pension plans**

Qualifying payments made in 1998-99	**14.6** £	1998-99 payments used in an earlier year	**14.7** £	**Relief claimed**
1998-99 payments now to be carried back	**14.8** £	Payments brought back from 1999-2000	**14.9** £	box 14.6 *minus* (boxes 14.7 and 14.8, but not 14.9) **14.10** £

- **Employee contributions to personal pension plans** (include your gross contribution - *see the note on box 14.11 in your Tax Return Guide*)

Qualifying payments made in 1998-99	**14.11** £	1998-99 payments used in an earlier year	**14.12** £	**Relief claimed**
1998-99 payments now to be carried back	**14.13** £	Payments brought back from 1999-2000	**14.14** £	box 14.11 *minus* (boxes 14.12 and 14.13, but not 14.14) **14.15** £

- **Contributions to other pension schemes**

- Amount of contributions to employer's schemes **not deducted** at source from pay   **14.16** £

- Gross amount of free-standing additional voluntary contributions paid in 1998-99   **14.17** £

What to enter
The amounts paid in the year ended 5 April 1999.

There are boxes to complete if you wish the pension contributions to be carried back to the 1997-98 tax year, or if you have already made a separate claim to carry back contributions. Contributions will only need to be entered in box 14.16 in exceptional circumstances.

FILL THIS IN IF:	**WHERE TO FIND THE INFORMATION**
You have a retirement annuity policy or personal pension plan.	The insurance company will provide a certificate of payments at the end of each tax year.

REMEMBER:

If you have paid contributions in excess of the maximum allowable for the year to 5 April 1999, you may be able to carry forward unused relief if you have paid less than maximum contributions in the previous six years. The table on page 15 shows the maximum contributions allowable for tax as a percentage of your earnings. You can request help sheet IR300 from the Inland Revenue orderline which includes a working sheet to help with your calculations.

Q15 Other reliefs you can claim

Tick the 'Yes' box if you want to claim for vocational training, interest on a loan to purchase your main home if it is outside MIRAS, other allowable interest payments, maintenance or alimony payments, Venture Capital Trust and Enterprise Investment Scheme Subscriptions, covenants to charities, Gift Aid, post cessation expenses or payments to a trade union or friendly society for death benefits.

If you do not wish to claim any of these, tick the 'No' box and move to Q16.

Q 15	**Do you want to claim any of the following reliefs?**	NO	YES	If yes, fill in boxes 15.1 to 15.12, as appropriate.

		Amount of payment
●	Payments you made for vocational training	15.1 £

FILL THIS IN IF:	**WHERE TO FIND THE INFORMATION**	**What to enter**
You have paid for a vocational training course leading to a NVQ or SVQ qualification and you are aged between 16 and 18, not in full-time education, or 19 and over. You must be resident in the U.K. and not receiving an educational loan or grant.	The training organisation will have given you a certificate confirming the payment and tax deduction.	The amount you have paid your training provider, which will be after deducting tax at basic rate. You should not complete this section if the course was undertaken primarily as a leisure activity.

		Amount of payment
●	Interest eligible for relief on loans to buy your main home (other than MIRAS)	15.2 £

What to enter
The amount of the interest paid on the first £30,000 of loans.

FILL THIS IN IF:

You paid interest *outside the MIRAS system* on a mortgage or loan to buy your main residence, or land on which to build one,and it is in the U.K. or Republic of Ireland; or had a bridging loan to facilitate the purchase and sale of such a house.

Also any interest paid *outside the MIRAS system* on loans taken out before 6 April 1988 if the loan was to improve a house, or buy a house that is occupied rent-free by a dependent relative who, by being incapacitated by old age or infirmity, is being maintained by you, or to buy a house for a former or separated husband or wife.

WHERE TO FIND THE INFORMATION

Ask the lender for an interest paid certificate for the year ended 5 April 1999.

Tax relief is restricted to 10 per cent and to the interest on the first £30,000 of loans. No higher rate relief is available.

(Tax relief was reduced from 15% to 10% from 6 April 1998.)

Allocation of interest – Multiple owners

The £30,000 limit applies to the *property* regardless of the number of borrowers. It is possible for several residents each to have a mortgage on the same house, but relief on the interest is still restricted to a maximum total loan amount of £30,000 on loans taken out after 31 July 1988. The maximum relief each owner of a property can have is £30,000 divided by the number of borrowers.

Owners must enter their own claim for relief in their own tax returns.

An owner who cannot use his or her full portion can transfer the difference for tax relief purposes to another owner of the same property.

Allocation of interest – Married couples

Regardless of whether the property or the mortgage is in the wife's or husband's name, then provided that it is the couple's main residence, mortgage interest paid (up to a maximum of £30,000 loan) can be allocated between the couple whichever way they choose to give the most beneficial tax advantage.

You can also vary the ratios from year to year by filling in form 15; this has to be sent to your tax office by 31 January, twenty-two months after the end of the tax year.

Tick the appropriate box in the return, and the tax office will send you the form to complete.

	Amount of payment
● Interest eligible for relief on other qualifying loans	**15.3** £

FILL THIS IN IF:

You pay interest on a loan which was used to buy shares in, or lend to:

A closely controlled trading company where you own more than 5 per cent of the company's shares, or, if less, have worked for the greater part of your time in the management of the company – such interest is not allowed for tax if a claim for relief has been made under the Enterprise Investment Scheme.

A partnership or employee-controlled company.

A co-operative, provided that you work in it full time.

Or you pay interest on a loan to pay inheritance tax or buy plant or machinery for business use.

Such interest is also allowed on loans to buy an annuity if the person buying the annuity is aged 65 or over when the loan is secured on the individual's main residence in the U.K. or Republic of Ireland.

What to enter
The gross amount actually paid.

WHERE TO FIND THE INFORMATION

Ask the lender for a certificate of interest from which you can obtain the figures to go in your return.

- Maintenance or alimony payments you have made under a court order, Child Support Agency assessment or legally binding order or agreement

Amount claimed under 'new' rules

15.4 £

Amount claimed under 'old' rules up to £1,900	Amount claimed under 'old' rules over £1,900
15.5 £	**15.6** £

What to enter

In box 15.4 state the amount you paid in the year ended 5 April 1999. The maximum figure for tax relief is £1,900 so you can only put the lower figure or £1,900 in the box.

If your Maintenance agreement is under the 'old' rules relief is on the lower of the amounts on which you received tax relief in 1988–89, or on the amount which was due and which you actually paid in 1998–99; if this figure is more than £1,900 you can only enter £1,900 in box 15.5 and the difference between this and £1,900 in box 15.6.

If less than £1,900 put the amount paid in box 15.5.

FILL THIS IN IF:

You make legally enforceable maintenance or alimony payments. Do not include voluntary payments for there is no tax relief for these.

WHERE TO FIND THE INFORMATION

You will know from your own records or from a court, DSS or Child Support Agency statement the payments made.

TAX TIP:

There are special rules and reliefs affecting maintenance payments to adults, and to children, if they are paid under a legally binding agreement made before 15 March 1988, or a court order applied for on or before that date but in place by 30 June 1988. In certain circumstances you can benefit by making an election to transfer to the current tax relief levels.

Ask your tax office for a new explanatory leaflet IR93.

- Subscriptions for Venture Capital Trust shares (up to £100,000)

Amount on which relief claimed

15.7 £

- Subscriptions under the Enterprise Investment Scheme (up to £150,000)

Amount on which relief claimed

15.8 £

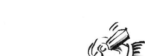

WHERE TO FIND THE INFORMATION

The trust or scheme will have given you a share certificate and a memorandum of the trust's status, etc. and a receipt for the amount paid.

In the case of the EIS you will receive a form EIS 3 or EIS 5 which the tax office may wish to see to support your claim.

You cannot claim tax relief until you have this form – if it arrives after you have submitted your tax return write to your tax office immediately.

FILL THIS IN IF:

You have subscribed for shares in a Venture Capital Trust or Enterprise Investment Scheme.

What to enter

The amount you subscribed up to the maximum.

Amount of payment

- Charitable covenants or annuities **15.9** £

FILL THIS IN IF:

You have signed a covenant to pay money to a charity for a period of at least four years or you are making covenanted payments for business reasons such as an annuity to a former partner.

WHERE TO FIND THE INFORMATION

You should have a copy of the covenant form you signed, or a note of the payments made.

What to enter

The net amount of the actual payments made. You will have deducted tax at basic rate before making the payments, so further tax relief is only available if you are a higher-rate taxpayer.

Amount of payment

- Gift Aid and Millennium Gift Aid **15.10** £

FILL THIS IN IF:

You have donated £250 or more net to a charity and signed a Gift Aid Certificate R190(SD) or donated £100 or more, including gifts made by instalments once they reach £100, to the Millennium Gift Aid between 31 July 1998 and 31 December 2000.

WHERE TO FIND THE INFORMATION

You should have a letter from the charity confirming the amount paid.

What to enter

The actual net amount paid; tax at the basic rate will have been deducted from the payment so further tax relief is available only if you are a higher-rate tax payer.

Amount of payment

- Post-cessation expenses and losses on relevant discounted securities etc. **15.11** £

FILL THIS IN IF:

You ceased trading within the last seven years but have still incurred expenditure closely related to that business.

WHERE TO FIND THE INFORMATION

From invoices, receipts, correspondence, etc.

What to enter

The amount of the relevant expenditure.

If your income in the year of payment is not sufficient to fully utilise the relief then a claim may be made for the excess to be treated as an allowable loss for capital gains tax purposes (see page 49).

	Half amount of payment
• Payments to a trade union or friendly society for death benefits	**15.12** £

FILL THIS IN IF:

You make compulsory payments to provide annuities for widows and orphans where relief is not given by your employer, or if part of your trade union subscription relates to a pension, insurance or funeral benefits, or you have a friendly society policy providing sickness and death benefits (the part relating to death benefit may qualify for tax relief).

WHERE TO FIND THE INFORMATION

The company or trade union operating the policies will provide you each year with a statement that will give you the figures required.

What to enter
One half of the payment made.

REMEMBER:

With self assessment tax legislation the law requires you to keep all records of earnings, income, benefits, profits, expenses, etc. and all other relevant information for 22 months from the end of the tax year if you are employed, and for 5 years and 10 months if you are self-employed.

REMEMBER:

Private medical insurance for people aged 60 or over

Tax relief on payments for private medical insurance for the over 60s was abolished in respect of **annual** contracts made or renewed on or after 2 July 1997. Tax relief is given by basic rate tax being deducted from the premium paid for existing contracts until they expire.

Q16 Your tax allowances for the year ending 5 April 1999

You automatically get the personal allowance each year if you are resident in the U.K. but all other allowances have to be claimed.

If you want to claim blind person's allowance, married couple's allowance, single person's allowance, widow's bereavement allowance or you wish to transfer surplus allowances between husband and wife, then tick the 'Yes' box. Otherwise tick the 'No' box and proceed to Q17.

ALLOWANCES *for the year ended 5 April 1999*

Q 16 You get your personal allowance of £4,195 automatically. **If you were born before 6 April 1934, enter your date of birth in box 21.4** - you may get higher age-related allowances.

Do you want to claim any of the following allowances? | NO | YES

If yes, please read pages 23 to 26 of your Tax Return Guide and then fill in boxes 16.1 to 16.28 as appropriate.

Date of registration (if first year of claim)		Local authority (or other register)
■ *Blind person's allowance*	16.1 / /	16.2

FILL THIS IN IF:

You are a registered blind person.

What to enter
The date you were registered blind if it is the first time you have claimed, and also the name of your local authority.

TAX TIP:

This allowance is also claimable by blind persons in the year *preceding* the year in which they were officially registered as blind if, at the end of the previous year, evidence was *then* available to support the eventual registration application.

■ *Transitional allowance* (for some wives with husbands on low income if received in earlier years).

● Tick to claim and give details in the 'Additional information' box on page 8
(please see page 23 of your Tax Return Guide for what is needed) | 16.3

● If you want to calculate your tax, enter the amount of transitional allowance you can have in box 16.4 | 16.4 £

FILL THIS IN IF:

You are a married woman and you were able to claim a transitional allowance in 1997–98 because your husband was on low income and your husband has written to his tax office asking for the allowance to be given to you.

What to enter
Ask your tax office to confirm the figure you should put in your tax return. You will need to enter your husband's name, NI number and tax reference in the additional information box on page 8 of the return.

■ *Married couple's allowance for a married man* - *see page 24 of your Tax Return Guide.*

- Wife's full name **16.5**

- Wife's date of birth (if before 6 April 1934) **16.7** / /

box number 16.9 is not used

- Date of marriage (if after 5 April 1998) **16.6** / /

- Tick box 16.8 if you or your wife have allocated **half** the allowance to her **16.8**

- Tick box 16.10 if you and your wife have allocated **all** the allowance to her **16.10**

FILL THIS IN IF:

You are a married man and you are living with your wife or separated before 6 April 1990 but you are still married to her and wholly maintaining her.

What to enter

Your wife's full name and date of birth if before 6 April 1934; also your date of marriage if it was during the tax year, and tick box 16.8 or 16.10 if you have agreed to allocate part or all of the allowance to your wife.

TAX TIP:

Who gets the married couple's allowance?

The allowance automatically goes to the husband unless either the husband or the wife has asked for one half to be given to each other (boxes 16.8 and 16.13) or both husband and wife have asked for the whole allowance to be given to the wife (boxes 16.10 and 16.15).

It is beneficial to transfer this allowance if it cannot be used fully by a husband.

Ask your tax office for Form 18 if you wish to transfer half, or all, of the married couple's allowance, but this has to be submitted before the tax year to which it relates so it is already too late for it to apply to the 1999-2000 tax year but see page 25 regarding surplus allowances.

■ *Married couple's allowance for a married woman* - *see page 24 of your Tax Return Guide.*

- Husband's full name **16.12**

box number 16.14 is not used

- Date of marriage (if after 5 April 1998) **16.11** / /

- Tick box 16.13 if you or your husband have allocated **half** the allowance to you **16.13**

- Tick box 16.15 if you and your husband have allocated **all** the allowance to you **16.15**

What to enter

Your husband's name, marriage date if in the last year and tick either box 16.13 or 16.15.

FILL THIS IN IF:

You are a married woman and have agreed with your husband to transfer half, or all, of the married couple's allowance (see above).

TAX TIP:

The Age-allowance trap

If you are married, over 65 and claiming Age allowance, estimate your total income for the next tax year to see that no personal allowance will remain unused; it may be beneficial to transfer savings, etc. into joint names.

■ *Additional personal allowance* (available in some circumstances if you have a child living with you - *see page 25 of your Tax Return Guide*).

● Tick box 16.16A if you are claiming the married couple's allowance **and** additional personal allowance because your spouse was unable to work, because of illness or disablement, throughout the year ended 5 April 1999 | 16.16A |

● Name of the child claimed for | 16.16 |

● Child's date of birth | 16.17 | / /

● Tick if child lives with you | 16.18 |

● Name of university etc/type of training if the child is 16 or over on 6 April 1998 and in full time education or training | 16.19 |

Sharing a claim

Name and address of other person claiming | 16.20 |

Postcode

● Enter your share as a percentage | 16.21 | %

● If share not agreed, enter the number of days in the year ended 5 April 1999 that the child lived with

- you | 16.22 | days

- other person | 16.23 | days

FILL THIS IN IF:

You are a one-parent family, or a married man looking after children because your wife is incapacitated, or a married woman with children and an incapacitated husband.

This allowance is given if your child is living with you and is under 16, or if older is receiving full-time education, or on a training course (including YTS) for at least two years. It is also given for a child under 18 who is not your child but who is living with and maintained by you.

What to enter

Give the child's name and date of birth and tick the box to confirm the child lives with you. Also state if the child is receiving full-time education if over 16. If you are claiming the allowance because your husband or wife was incapacitated throughout the tax year, tick box 16.16A

In the case of shared claims, give the details requested.

■ *Widow's bereavement allowance*

● Date of your husband's death | 16.24 | / /

FILL THIS IN IF:

You are a widow and your husband has died since 6 April 1997.

Widows are entitled to an additional tax allowance in the year of bereavement and any unused married couple's allowance for the year of the husband's death can also be claimed. The additional personal allowance is also available if applicable.

The allowance is also available in the following tax year unless you remarried before it began.

What to enter

The date of your husband's death.

■ *Transfer of surplus allowances* - *see page 26 of your Tax Return Guide before you fill in boxes 16.25 to 16.28.*

● Tick if you want your spouse to have your unused allowances **16.25**

● Tick if you want to have your spouse's unused allowances **16.26**

Please give details in the 'Additional information' box on page 8 - *see page 26 of your Tax Return Guide for what is needed.*

If you want to calculate your tax, enter the amount of the surplus allowance you can have.

● Blind person's **surplus** allowance **16.27** £

● Married couple's **surplus** allowance **16.28** £

FILL THIS IN IF:

You are unable to use all your married couple's allowance or blind person's allowance and wish to transfer one surplus to your husband or wife.

What to enter

If you have surplus allowances to transfer tick box 16.25 and if you are claiming surplus allowances tick box 16.26. You may also add your calculation of the surplus allowances available if you wish.

Q17 Other information

Answer 'Yes' or 'No' as to whether you received a tax refund in the year ended 5 April 1999. If 'Yes' state the amount.

OTHER INFORMATION *for the year ended 5 April 1999*

Q17 ▶ **Have you already had any 1998-99 tax refunded or set off by your Tax Office or the DSS Benefits Agency?** *Read the notes for box 17.1 on page 26 of your Tax Return Guide*

NO | **YES**

If yes, enter the amount of the refund in box 17.1.

17.1 £

Q18 Do you want to calculate your tax?

If you **do not** want to calculate your own tax liability or tax refund and you would prefer the tax office to do it for you, just tick 'No' and go on to Q19.

If you **do** want to do it yourself, then tick 'Yes' and complete the boxes as shown.

Q18 ▶ **Do you want to calculate your tax?**

NO | **YES**

If yes, do it now and then fill in boxes 18.1 to 18.9. Your Tax Calculation Guide will help.

● Unpaid tax for earlier years **included in your tax code for 1998-99** — **18.1** £

● Tax due for 1998-99 included in your tax code for a later year — **18.2** £

● Total tax and Class 4 NIC due for 1998-99 **before** you made any payments on account *(put the amount in brackets if an overpayment)* — **18.3** £

● Tax due for earlier years — **18.4** £

● Tick box 18.5 if you have calculated tax overpaid for earlier years (and enter the amount in the 'Additional information' box on page 8 — **18.5**

● Your first payment on account for 1999-2000 *(include the pence)* — **18.6** £

Tick box 18.7 if you are making a claim to reduce your 1999-2000 payments on account and say why in the 'Additional information' box **18.7**

Tick box 18.8 if you do **not** need to make 1999-2000 payments on account — **18.8**

● 1999-2000 tax you are reclaiming now — **18.9** £

FILL THIS IN IF:

You want to calculate your own tax.

What to enter

You need to turn to page 64 of this book to complete Your Tax Calculation Sheets then you can complete boxes 18.1 to 18.9.

Q19 Do you want to claim a tax repayment?

If you are due a tax repayment and you **don't** want it offset against your next tax bill, or through your PAYE code number, then tick 'Yes' and fill in the information requested – otherwise tick 'No'. If you do not claim a repayment but one is due to you then the tax office will set any amount to be refunded against your next tax bill. Now proceed to Q20 and Q21.

| Q19 | **Do you want to claim a repayment if you have paid too much tax?** *(If you tick 'No' or the tax you have overpaid is below £10, I will use the amount you are owed to reduce your next tax bill.)* | **NO** | **YES** | If yes, fill in boxes 19.1 to 19.12 as appropriate. |

Should the repayment (or payment) be sent:

- to you? *Tick box 19.1* **19.1**

or

- to your bank or building society account or other nominee? *Tick box 19.2* **19.2**

If you ticked either box 19.2 or 19.9, fill in boxes 19.3 to 19.8, 19.11 and 19.12 as appropriate.

Your (or your nominee's) bank or building society **19.3**

Branch sort code **19.4** – –

Account number **19.5**

Name of account **19.6**

Building society ref. **19.7**

If your nominee is your agent, *tick box 19.9 and complete boxes 19.10 to 19.12* **19.9**

Agent's ref. for you **19.10**

Name of your nominee/agent

I authorise **19.8**

Nominee's address **19.11**

Postcode

to receive on my behalf the amount due

This authority must be signed by you. A photocopy of your signature will not do. **19.12**

Signature

Q20 and Q21 Check your personal details

Check that your name, address and reference number on the front page of your tax form are correct and complete boxes 21.1 to 21.6, then proceed to Q22. You do not **have** to state a telephone number but it could save the tax office and you having to write letters to sort out a minor problem or misunderstanding. Entries in boxes 21.5 and 21.6 are only required if you are self-employed

| Q20 | **Are your details on the front of the Tax Return wrong?** | **NO** | **YES** | If yes, please make any corrections on the front of the form. |

| Q21 | **Please give other personal details in boxes 21.1 to 21.6** *This information helps us to be more efficient and effective and may support claims you have made elsewhere in your Tax Return* |

Please give a daytime telephone number if convenient. It is often simpler to phone if we need to ask you about your Tax Return.

Your telephone number or, if you prefer, your agent's telephone number **21.1**

21.2

(also give your agent's name and reference in the 'Additional information' box on page 8)

Enter your first two forenames **21.5**

Say if you are single, married, widowed, divorced or separated **21.3**

Date of birth **21.4** / /

Enter your date of birth if you are self-employed, or you were born before 6 April 1934, or you have ticked the 'Yes' box in Question 14, or you are claiming relief for Venture Capital Trust subscriptions

Enter your National Insurance number (if known) **21.6**

Q22 and Q23 Additional information and declaration

OTHER INFORMATION *for the year ended 5 April 1999, continued*

Q22 Please tick boxes 22.1 to 22.5 if they apply and provide any additional information in the box below.

Tick box 22.1 if you expect to receive a new pension or Social Security benefit in 1999-2000. **22.1**

Tick box 22.2 if you do **not** want any tax you owe for 1998-99 collected through your tax code. **22.2**

Tick box 22.3 if this Tax Return contains figures that are provisional because you do not yet have final figures. Give details below. Page 27 of your Tax Return Guide explains the circumstances in which Tax Returns containing provisional figures may be accepted. **22.3**

box number 22.4 is not used

Tick box 22.5 if you want to claim:

- relief now for 1999-2000 trading or certain capital losses. Enter the amount and year in the 'Additional information' box below
- to have post-cessation or other business receipts taxed as income of an earlier year. Enter the amount and year in the 'Additional information' box below
- backwards or forwards spreading of literary or artistic income. Enter in the 'Additional information' box details of any amounts spread back to last year and, if appropriate, the year before
- for a payment to your employer's compulsory widow's, widower's or orphan's benefit scheme (available in some circumstances – read the notes on page 27 of your Tax Return Guide **before** you tick the box). Enter the amount, in terms of tax, in the 'Additional information' box below. **22.5**

Additional information

Your tax office needs the above information in order to ensure that your tax affairs are dealt with efficiently; if there is insufficient room use the additional information box on page 8. You must then sign and date the Declaration Q23 ensuring that you have ticked the boxes to indicate which sections of the tax return you have completed and are returning.

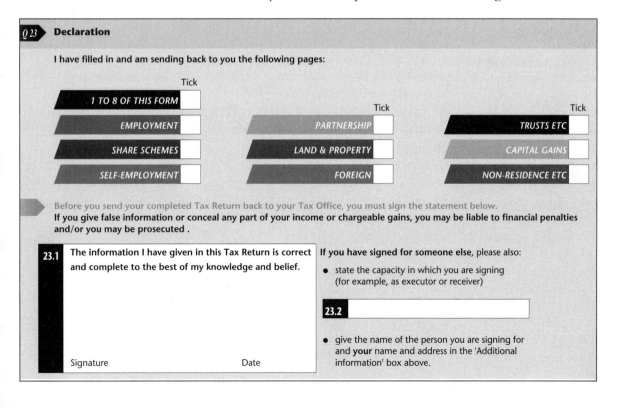

Q23 Declaration

I have filled in and am sending back to you the following pages:

	Tick		Tick		Tick
1 TO 8 OF THIS FORM					
EMPLOYMENT		PARTNERSHIP		TRUSTS ETC	
SHARE SCHEMES		LAND & PROPERTY		CAPITAL GAINS	
SELF-EMPLOYMENT		FOREIGN		NON-RESIDENCE ETC	

Before you send your completed Tax Return back to your Tax Office, you must sign the statement below.
If you give false information or conceal any part of your income or chargeable gains, you may be liable to financial penalties and/or you may be prosecuted .

23.1 The information I have given in this Tax Return is correct and complete to the best of my knowledge and belief.

If you have signed for someone else, please also:
- state the capacity in which you are signing (for example, as executor or receiver)

23.2

- give the name of the person you are signing for and **your** name and address in the 'Additional information' box above.

Signature   Date

What to do when you have completed your tax return

Sign the return and keep a copy

When you sign your tax return you are declaring that to the best of your knowledge and belief the return is complete, true and accurate.

It is often thought that if you keep quiet about some of your income, then the tax inspector will not find out about it. This is not the case. The tax authorities have many sources of information, the most common being your employer, banks, building societies and other businesses, all of whom may be required to make a return of payments made to individuals and businesses.

If you forget to include some of your income on the form you should immediately notify your tax office explaining your error.

REMEMBER:

You will only have entered **total** figures in the boxes on your tax return, so ensure that you keep a note of how you arrived at the figures – the tax office may ask for them.

TAX TIP:

Do not worry if you have forgotten to claim an allowance due to you, for you have a time limit of six years in which to tell your tax office of your mistake.
Therefore you can go back to 6 April 1992 to check your tax and possibly get a rebate – and interest too.

You should keep a copy of your completed tax return form so that, at a later date, you can check your PAYE code or the amount of tax you have paid. If you fill in the tax forms reproduced in this book you will have a permanent record.

When to send in your tax return

If you don't want to calculate your own tax:

You need to send in your tax return by 30 September 1999 – the tax office should then send you a statement by 31 January 2000. This form SA302 'Self assessment – Tax Calculation for 1998–99' will either agree your figures or identify corrections that the tax office have made. If you disagree with the tax office's comments write to them; otherwise pay the amount demanded.

If you do want to calculate your own tax:

If you wish to use the tax calculator and calculate your own tax liability (see page 64) then you have until 31 January 2000 to send in your return, in which case you should also pay the tax that you think is due.

If you miss the date?

If you send in your return after 30 September 1999 (and *you* don't want to calculate your own tax) the tax office will not guarantee to calculate it for you before 31 January; they will still send you, however, a demand for a payment on account on 31 January, so *you* need to know approximately what your tax liability is in total.

Payments on Account

If you have enough untaxed income, or are self-employed, you will have to make two payments on account for each tax year, e.g. for the year ended 5 April 1999 the first payment for 50 per cent of your expected tax bill on 31 January 1999 and the second 50 per cent on 31 July 1999; any balance due (or refund), once your tax liability is agreed, is payable on 31 January 2000. (Self-employed payments will also include Class 4 National Insurance liability.) It is up to you to work out how much you need to pay on account.

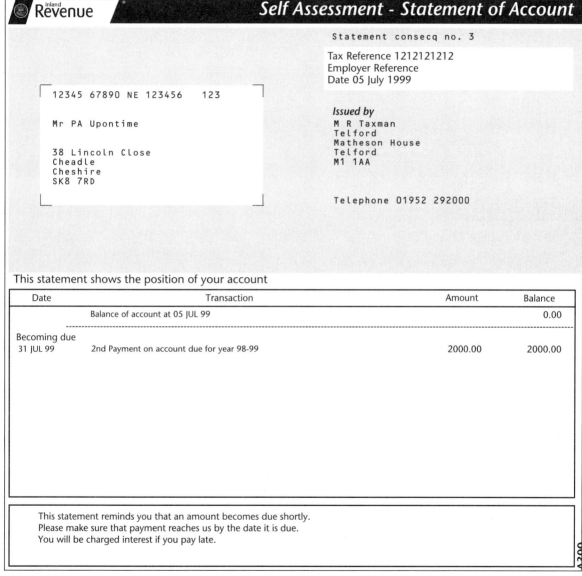

If You Receive This Form

Form SA300 above is an example of a demand for payment of tax – either on account or for a specific tax liability.

If you agree with the figure, you should pay the amount by the date shown. If it is wrong, ask for Form SA303. (See page 30).

Inland Revenue	Self Assessment	Claim to reduce payments on account

If this reference box is blank please give your Tax reference, Employer reference or National Insurance number. You will find this information, together with the name and address of your Tax Office, in the top right hand corner of your Statement of Account.

Tax reference
Employer reference
National Insurance number

Tax Office name and address

Please read the notes overleaf before completing this form

Name of taxpayer

Tax year to which this claim relates [—] Example, enter the tax year ending 5 April 1999 as [1998 — 99]

I believe that

√ [ ] the total Income Tax and Class 4 NIC payable for the tax year of claim (less any tax deducted at source and tax credits on dividends) will be less than the total of the payments on account based on the liability for the previous tax year

or

√ [ ] there will be no liability to any Income Tax or Class 4 NIC for the tax year of claim

My reason(s)
√

[ ] the taxable business profits for the tax year of claim are less than in the previous tax year

[ ] the tax allowances and reliefs for the tax year of claim are more than in the previous tax year

[ ] the tax deducted at source for the tax year of claim is more than in the previous tax year

[ ] the taxable income (after allowances) for the tax year of claim is less than in the previous tax year

[ ] other reason *please specify*

I wish to reduce each of the payments on account for the tax year of claim to £ [   ]

*Each reduced payment on account should be **half** of the net Income Tax and Class 4 NIC you expect to have to pay for the tax year.*

I understand that

• **if the payments on account finally due are greater than the amounts paid, interest will be payable on the difference**

• **any incorrect statement made fraudulently or negligently in connection with this claim could incur a penalty.**

Date [   ]

Signed [   ]

Agent's Name *if signed by agent* [   ]

Agent's Reference [   ]

When you have completed and signed this form send it to your Tax Office.

FILL THIS IN IF:

You wish to reduce the amount of tax being demanded on account. You must fill in the appropriate boxes on this form so that the tax office understand why you are claiming a reduction.

Send the completed form to your tax office, together with a cheque for the revised payment on account.

Your tax return – supplementary pages

EMPLOYMENT

You need to fill in this part of the tax return if you are employed. It will cover your income and benefits from employment and your claim for expenses for the year ended 5 April 1999. You must use a separate form for each employment. (Ministers of Religion and Members of Parliament have different versions of this form.)

Income for the year ended 5 April 1999

Inland Revenue

EMPLOYMENT

Details of employer

Employer's PAYE reference
1.1

Employer's name
1.2

Date employment started
(only if between 6 April 1998 and 5 April 1999)
1.3 / /

Employer's address
1.5

Date finished (only if between 6 April 1998 and 5 April 1999)
1.4 / /

Postcode

Tick box 1.6 if you were a director of the company
1.6

and, if so, tick box 1.7 if it was a close company
1.7

Income from employment

■ *Money* - see Notes, page EN3

Before tax

● Payments from P60 (or P45 or pay slips)   **1.8** £

● Payments not on P60 etc.   - tips   **1.9** £

  - other payments (excluding expenses shown below and lump sums and compensation payments or benefits shown overleaf)   **1.10** £

Tax deducted

● UK tax deducted from payments in boxes 1.8 to 1.10   **1.11** £

WHERE TO FIND THE INFORMATION

By law, your employer has to give you a P60 form (certificate of pay, income tax and national insurance) by 31 May 1999 (see page 58). This will show the earnings figures to go in your tax return.

Alternatively, you may need to refer to a P45 form or your pay slips.

FILL THIS IN IF:

You are an employee or a director, and receive a salary, wages or benefits.

What to enter

Fill in boxes 1.1 to 1.7 with the information requested. In box 1.8 show the amount you have received *before* any deductions for income tax or national insurance.

You *are* allowed to subtract any deduction made by your employer for contributions to an approved pension scheme or payroll giving donations.

Enter in box 1.9 any tips or gratuities you have received if they are *not* included in the figure in box 1.8.

Box 1.10 is for any other payments, although most of them will be specifically referred to later in this form.

Enter any tax deducted in box 1.11.

Benefits and expenses - see Notes, pages EN3 to EN6. If any benefits connected with termination of employment were received, or enjoyed, after that termination and were from a **former** employer you need to complete Help Sheet IR204, available from the Orderline. Do not enter such benefits here.

- Assets transferred/ payments made for you — **1.12** £ *(Amount)*
- Vans — **1.18** £ *(Amount)*
- Vouchers/credit cards — **1.13** £ *(Amount)*
- Interest-free and low-interest loans — **1.19** £ *(Amount)*
- Living accommodation — **1.14** £ *(Amount)*
- Mobile telephones — **1.20** £ *(Amount)*
- Mileage allowance — **1.15** £ *(Amount)*
- Private medical or dental insurance — **1.21** £ *(Amount)*
- Company cars — **1.16** £ *(Amount)*
- Other benefits — **1.22** £ *(Amount)*
- Fuel for company cars — **1.17** £ *(Amount)*
- Expenses payments received and balancing charges — **1.23** £ *(Amount)*

FILL THIS IN IF:

You have received any 'benefits' from your employer. Typically those might include private health cover, a low interest loan, or a mobile phone.

or

Your employer has provided you, or your family, with a car available for your private use.

or

Your employer has either paid directly or reimbursed any expenses relating to your employment.

To find out if your benefit is taxable, turn to page 63 of this book.

WHERE TO FIND THE INFORMATION

Most of the information will be found on the P11D form, a copy of which your employer must by law give you by 6 July 1999. For an explanation of how car and fuel benefits are calculated, see page 61.

Is the benefit taxable?

All employees and directors whose earnings, including expenses and benefits in kind, are at a rate of £8,500 or more a year are liable to pay tax on benefits and expenses received.

Certain benefits are taxable on all employees.

The car benefit tax applies to all company cars, including those that are leased.

See page 34 for tax relief you can claim in respect of genuine business expenditure.

What to enter

The amount paid to you as a benefit or expense or the taxable value.

If your employer has agreed with the tax office that certain expenses need not be shown as you would be entitled to tax relief for the full amount (e.g. representatives' overnight stays; mileage allowances for your own car used on business), then your employer should give you details of the expenses covered by the arrangement.

Income from employment continued

■ *Lump sums and compensation payments or benefits including such payments and benefits from a former employer*
Note that 'lump sums' here includes any contributions which your employer made to an unapproved retirement benefits scheme

*You must read page EN6 of the Notes **before** filling in boxes 1.24 to 1.30*

Reliefs

- £30,000 exemption **1.24** £
- Foreign service and disability **1.25** £
- Retirement and death lump sums **1.26** £

Taxable lump sums

- From box H of *Help Sheet IR204* **1.27** £
- From box Q of *Help Sheet IR204* **1.28** £
- From box R of *Help Sheet IR204* **1.29** £

Tax deducted
- Tax deducted from payments in boxes 1.27 to 1.29 **1.30** £

FILL THIS IN IF:	WHERE TO FIND THE INFORMATION
You have been made redundant or dismissed with compensation.	You will find the information in a letter or statement from your employer.

What to enter
You will need Inland Revenue Help Sheet IR204 to assist you in filling in these boxes. If it has not been sent then telephone 0645 000404 for a copy.

DO NOT FILL THIS IN IF:	WARNING
The amount you received has had tax deducted from it and it is included in the figures on your P60 form included in box 1.8 on page 31.	If your contract of employment gives you a right to compensation on ceasing to be employed, then the lump sums you receive will be taxable, regardless of the amount.

Is it taxable?
The first £30,000 of compensation is tax free but any amount in excess of that figure is taxable at your highest individual rate of tax.

■ *Foreign earnings not taxable in the UK in year ended 5 April 1999* - see Notes, page EN6   **1.31** £

FILL THIS IN IF:
You are non-resident (see page 51) or have reason to believe such income is not liable to U.K. tax.

What to enter
That part of your income that you think is not taxable in the U.K.

■ *Expenses you incurred in doing your job* - *see Notes, starting on page EN6*

- Travel and subsistence costs **1.32** £
- Fixed deductions for expenses **1.33** £
- Professional fees and subscriptions **1.34** £
- Other expenses and capital allowances **1.35** £
- Tick box 1.36 if the figure in box 1.32 includes travel between your home and a permanent workplace **1.36**

FILL THIS IN IF:

Your employer has reimbursed business expenses or you have paid an expense that has not been reimbursed by your employer without which you would have been unable to do your job properly (the tax law says it must be 'wholly, exclusively and necessary for your employment'). You may be able to get a letter from your employer confirming this.

What to enter

The amount of the expense in the appropriate box (see page 39 in respect of capital allowances). You should not send any receipts with your tax return but you should keep them in case the tax office ask for them.

TAX TIP:

You could consider claiming for:

Extra clothing costs, tools, trade journals and technical books if you are a factory or manual worker, or if greater than any fixed allowance agreed between your trade union and the Inland Revenue.

Travelling and subsistence expenses (other than to your main place of employment).

The cost of business mileage travelled in your own car may be claimed at a special rate, request leaflet IR125 and see page 61.

Use of a room at your home set aside as an office may be claimed based on a proportion of your outgoings if you have to do additional work at home.

Fees, subscriptions and journals to professional bodies, etc.

Entertaining business customers and business telephone calls.

■ *Foreign Earnings Deduction* **1.37** £

■ *Foreign tax for which tax credit relief not claimed* **1.38** £

FILL THIS IN IF:

You are a seafarer. (This general foreign earnings deduction was withdrawn as from 17 March 1998 for all other employees.)

WHERE TO FIND THE INFORMATION

The rules are very complicated so ask your tax office for more information by ringing 0645 000404 and requesting Help Sheet IR205.

SHARE SCHEMES

You need to fill in these pages if you received any share options or share-related benefits.

[Form image: Inland Revenue Share Schemes form with Share options and Shares acquired sections, boxes 2.1 to 2.48]

WHERE TO FIND THE INFORMATION

Refer to share option certificates, and correspondence from your Scheme's Trustees.

You may also need to know the market value of shares at relevant dates – your employer should be able to supply this information.

FILL THESE IN IF:

You received any share options or share-related benefits from your employer.

You have to complete a separate sheet for each taxable event – telephone the Inland Revenue order line on 0645 000404 if you require another form.

Also ask for Inland Revenue Help Sheet IR218 which will give further advice.

What to enter

Fill in the boxes appropriate to your share scheme. Rules and regulations vary from scheme to scheme; if you require help or advice before filling in the boxes consult your employer or the Trustees of your scheme.

If you have made any capital gains or losses do not enter them in this section – ask for supplementary pages **Capital Gains.**

SELF-EMPLOYMENT

You need to fill in this part of the tax return if you are self-employed but not in a partnership. (If you are in a Partnership, then you need the Partnership supplementary pages – see page 42).

Telephone the Inland Revenue order line on 0645 000404 if you need either of the forms – you need to fill in a separate set of pages for each business.

Income for the year ended 5 April 1999

Inland Revenue

SELF-EMPLOYMENT

*If you have answered 'Yes' to Question 3, fill in these Pages. You should read page SEN2 of the Notes on Self-employment **before** you start to fill in these Pages. The Notes are colour coded to match this form. If you were a Name at Lloyd's, fill in the Lloyd's Underwriters Pages instead.*

Pages SEN1 and SEN2 of the Notes tell you when you may **need to complete more than one** set of Self-employment Pages

Business details

Name of business
3.1

Description of business
3.2

Address of business
3.3

Postcode

Accounting period - *read the Notes, page SEN2 before filling in these boxes*

Start
3.4 / /

End
3.5 / /

- Tick box 3.5A if you entered details for all relevant accounting periods on last year's Tax Return and boxes 3.11 to 3.70 will be blank **3.5A**

- Tick box 3.6 if details in boxes 3.1 or 3.3 have changed since your last Tax Return **3.6**

- Tick box 3.7 if your accounts do not cover the period from the last accounting date (explain why in the 'Additional information' box below) **3.7**

- Tick box 3.8A if your accounting date has changed (only if this is a permanent change and you want it to count for tax) **3.8A**

- Tick box 3.8B if this is the second or further change (explain why you have not used the same date as last year in the 'Additional information' box) **3.8B**

- Date of commencement if after 5 April 1996 **3.9** / /

- Date of cessation if before 6 April 1999 **3.10** / /

Additional information

FILL THIS IN IF:

You get income from work done on a self-employed or freelance basis, or you let rooms furnished and provide services so that it is considered as a 'trade' but *not* if you are in partnership,.

What to enter

State the kind of work you do and your business name and address (it may be your normal name or a trading name) and fill in boxes 3.4 and 3.5 with the relevant dates.

Boxes 3.5A and 3.8B need ticking where relevant – they are designed to let the tax office know of any change in accounting dates. Tick box 3.9 if you have started in business since 6 April 1996, and fill in 3.10 if you have ceased trading.

Income and expenses - annual turnover below £15,000

*If your annual turnover is £15,000 or more, **ignore** boxes 3.11 to 3.13.* *Now fill in Page SE2*

*If your annual turnover is below £15,000, **fill in boxes 3.11 to 3.13 instead of Page SE2**. Read the Notes, page SEN2.*

- Turnover, other business receipts and goods etc. taken for personal use (and balancing charges) **3.11** £
- Expenses allowable for tax (including capital allowances) **3.12** £

box 3.11 *minus* box 3.12

Net profit (put figure in brackets if a loss) **3.13** £

What to enter
You only need to give three figures: your turnover, allowable expenses and profit (or loss). Obviously you will have prepared your own accounts in order to obtain these figures.

It is not necessary to send them to the tax office with your tax return but you must keep them so that you can answer any queries that they may raise.

FILL THIS IN IF:

Your business turnover is less than £15,000 a year.

DO NOT FILL THIS IN IF:

Your miscellaneous income from self-employment is from a one-off freelance or spare time activity. You have to declare this income under Miscellaneous Income (see page 15 of this book).

Having filled in this section, now turn to box 3.61 (page 39 in this book) or if your turnover is **more** than £15,000 fill in the following sections.

Income and expenses - annual turnover £15,000 or more

You must fill in this Page if your annual turnover is £15,000 or more - read the Notes, page SEN2

If you were registered for VAT, do the figures in boxes 3.16 to 3.51, include VAT? **3.14** ☐ or exclude VAT? **3.15** ☐

Sales/business income (turnover)

3.16 £

	Disallowable expenses included in boxes 3.33 to 3.50	Total expenses
Cost of sales	**3.17** £	**3.33** £
Construction industry subcontractor costs	**3.18** £	**3.34** £
Other direct costs	**3.19** £	**3.35** £

box 3.16 *minus* (box 3.33 + box 3.34 + box 3.35)

Gross profit/(loss) **3.36** £

Other income/profits **3.37** £

Employee costs	**3.20** £	**3.38** £
Premises costs	**3.21** £	**3.39** £
Repairs	**3.22** £	**3.40** £
General administrative expenses	**3.23** £	**3.41** £
Motor expenses	**3.24** £	**3.42** £

• Travel and subsistence	**3.25** £		**3.43** £	
• Advertising, promotion and entertainment	**3.26** £		**3.44** £	
• Legal and professional costs	**3.27** £		**3.45** £	
• Bad debts	**3.28** £		**3.46** £	
• Interest	**3.29** £		**3.47** £	
• Other finance charges	**3.30** £		**3.48** £	
• Depreciation and loss/(profit) on sale	**3.31** £		**3.49** £	
• Other expenses	**3.32** £		**3.50** £	

Put the total of boxes 3.17 to 3.32 in **box 3.53 below**

total of boxes 3.38 to 3.50

Total expenses **3.51** £

boxes 3.36 + 3.37 *minus* box 3.51

Net profit/(loss) **3.52** £

What to enter

Not all the expenditure shown in your financial accounts will be allowable for tax against profits which is why there are two columns of figures – the left hand column (3.17 to 3.32) identifying any amounts that are disallowable; the figures to go in the right hand column (3.33 to 3.50) are those shown in your accounts.

FILL THIS IN IF:

Your business turnover is *more* than £15,000 a year.
(See also boxes 3.14 to 3.37 on the previous page.)

WHERE TO FIND THE INFORMATION

Your financial accounts and records should provide these figures.

Tax adjustments to net profit or loss

	total of boxes 3.17 to 3.32	
• Disallowable expenses	**3.53** £	
• Goods etc. taken for personal use and other adjustments (apart from disallowable expenses) that increase profits	**3.54** £	
• Balancing charges	**3.55** £	boxes 3.53 + 3.54 + 3.55
Total additions to net profit (deduct from net loss)		**3.56** £
• Capital allowances	**3.57** £	boxes 3.57 + 3.58
• Deductions from net profit (add to net loss)	**3.58** £	**3.59** £
		boxes 3.52 + 3.56 *minus* box 3.59
Net business profit for tax purposes (put figure in brackets if a loss)		**3.60** £

FILL THIS IN IF:

Your turnover is above £15,000 a year and you have completed boxes 3.14 to 3.52.

What to enter

The total disallowable expenses (box 3.53) shown above; an estimate of goods, etc. used personally (box 3.54). Box 3.55 is for any balancing charge (see page 39); Box 3.57 totals your capital allowances (see next page); Box 3.58 is for any amounts included in your accounts which are either not taxable or not relevant to your business (it is more likely that you will have covered these in the disallowable items on the previous page). Complete the remaining boxes.

Capital allowances - summary

	Capital allowances	Balancing charge
● Motor cars (Separate calculations must be made for each motor car costing more than £12,000 and for cars used partly for private motoring.)	**3.61** £	**3.62** £
● Other business plant and machinery	**3.63** £	**3.64** £
● Agricultural or Industrial Buildings Allowance (A separate calculation must be made for each block of expenditure.)	**3.65** £	**3.66** £
● Other capital allowances claimed (Separate calculations must be made.)	**3.67** £	**3.68** £
	total of column above	total of column above
Total capital allowances/balancing charges	**3.69** £	**3.70** £

What to enter

Any depreciation shown in your accounts will have been added back as disallowable in the earlier sections of this form; instead you can claim capital allowances. (A balancing charge arises if you sell an asset for more than its tax written down value – that is its original cost less cumulative capital allowances claimed).

FILL THIS IN IF:

You wish to claim capital allowances – regardless of your turnover level.

Table of Capital Allowances	*Writing down allowance %*
	on reducing balance
Plant, machinery and equipment*	25
Fixtures and fittings	25
Motor cars (maximum £3,000 a year)	25
Vans and lorries	25
Office furniture and equipment	25
Insulation of factories and warehouses	25
Fire safety expenditure	25
	on cost
Factories and warehouses	4
Agricultural buildings	4
Hotel buildings	4
Houses under assured tenancies scheme	4

All the above rates are doubled in respect of new investment in plant and machinery other than cars, etc. by small and medium-sized businesses in the 12 months ended 1 July 1998. For the period 2 July 1998 to 1 July 1999 the first year allowance is reduced from 50% to 40%.

*The annual rate of writing down allowance is reduced to 6% for most assets with a working life of 25 years or more purchased, or contracted, on or after 26 November 1996, but this applies only to businesses which spend more than £100,000 a year on such assets. For small/medium sized businesses this allowance was increased to 12% for new investment in the 12 months ended 1 July 1998.

Notes: There are higher allowances for buildings in enterprise zones, scientific research and film production expenditure, and special provisions for patent rights, know how, mines, mineral rights and certain other assets. Different rules apply to expenditure on plant and machinery for use in Northern Ireland.

The total allowances claimed can never exceed the cost of the asset.

Adjustments to arrive at taxable profit or loss

Basis period begins **3.71** / / and ends **3.72** / /

- Tick box 3.72A if the figure in box 3.88 is provisional **3.72A** [ ]

- Tick box 3.72B if the special arrangements for certain trades detailed in the guidance notes apply **3.72B** [ ]

Profit or loss of this account for tax purposes (box 3.13 or 3.60) **3.73** £

Adjustment to arrive at profit or loss for this basis period **3.74** £

- Overlap profit brought forward **3.75** £   • Deduct overlap relief used this year **3.76** £

- Overlap profit carried forward **3.77** £

Adjustment for farmers' averaging (see Notes, page SEN8 if you made a loss for 1998-99) **3.78** £

Net profit for 1998-99 (if loss, enter '0') **3.79** £

Allowable loss for 1998-99 (if you make a profit, enter '0') **3.80** £

- Loss offset against other income for 1998-99 **3.81** £

- Loss to carry back **3.82** £

- Loss to carry forward
  (that is allowable loss not claimed in any other way) **3.83** £

- Losses brought forward from last year **3.84** £

- Losses brought forward from last year used this year **3.85** £

box 3.79 *minus* box 3.85

Taxable profit after losses brought forward **3.86** £

- Any other business income (for example, Business Start-up Allowance received in 1998-99) **3.87** £

box 3.86 + box 3.87

Total taxable profits from this business **3.88** £

FILL THIS IN IF:

You have completed any of the sections of these supplementary pages so far. (See also boxes on the previous page.)

What to enter

The total (where applicable) from boxes completed on previous pages. Carry forward your overlap profit from box 3.77 of last year's return to box 3.75 of this return. (Ask for Help Sheet IR222 from the Inland Revenue.)

REMEMBER (Historical note!):

1996–97 was a transitional year in which the basis of tax assessment was changed. Until 1995–96 existing businesses had their tax assessment based on profits earned in their accounting year that ended in the *previous* tax year (5 April) – the 'preceding year' basis. This changed in 1996–97 so that current year's profits were accounted for and taxed in the year in which they were incurred – the 'current year' basis.

Your taxable profits for 1996–97 were calculated on the *average* of the current year's and previous year's profits; 1997–98 profits are based on your accounts period ending within the year ended 5 April 1998 and 1998-99 profits will be based on your accounts period ending within the year ended 5 April 1999.

There are special rules governing new businesses and those that have ceased trading.

Class 4 National Insurance Contributions

• Tick this box if exception or deferment applies	**3.89**	
• Adjustments to profit chargeable to Class 4 National Insurance Contributions	**3.90** £	
Class 4 National Insurance Contributions due	**3.91** £	

FILL THIS IN IF:

You are self-employed and you are liable to pay the full Class 4 National Insurance Contribution or if your liability might be reduced for some reason. Class 4 NI contribution is normally based on 6% of your taxable profit figure (after deducting capital allowances but including any enterprise allowance received), between £7,310 and £25,220 for 1998–99.

What to enter

Write in the reason for the deduction and the amounts.

Reasons for exemption or deferment may be due to your age, profit levels, infirmity, or it may be that you have made a loss, or have brought forward a loss from a previous year or have interest payments that will reduce your profits.

Subcontractors in the construction industry

• Deductions made by contractors on account of tax (you must send your SC60s to us)	**3.92** £	

FILL THIS IN IF:

You are a subcontractor in the building industry and have received any payments under that industry's tax deduction scheme.

What to enter

The amounts shown on forms SC60 which should be sent in with your tax return.

Summary of balance sheet

Leave these boxes blank if you do not have a balance sheet

■ **Assets**	• Plant, machinery and motor vehicles	**3.93** £	
	• Other fixed assets (premises, goodwill, investments etc.)	**3.94** £	
	• Stock and work in progress	**3.95** £	

FILL THIS IN IF:

Your turnover is over £15,000 and you are submitting a balance sheet with your profit and loss account.

What to enter

The figures, suitably grouped, from your accounts.

Note: The whole of the balance sheet boxes are not shown here – they extend to 3.109. In box 3.120 include any income received in your trade which has had tax deducted at source but exclude deductions made by contractors on account of tax.

PARTNERSHIPS

There are two types of partnership tax returns – short and long. Most partnerships will use the short version as their only partnership income will be trading income or taxed income from banks, building societies or deposit takers.

Income for the year ended 5 April 1999

Inland Revenue

PARTNERSHIP (SHORT)

If you have answered 'Yes' to Question 4, fill in Pages P1 and P2. If you want help, look up the box number in the Notes on Partnership at the back of your Tax Return Guide. They are colour-coded to match the form.

You can use these Short Pages if your only partnership income for the year was trading income or taxed interest from banks, building societies and deposit takers (you will see that box numbers do not run consecutively throughout - missing numbers are in the full version of the Partnership Pages). Otherwise you will need the Full Pages, available from the Orderline. You will need to fill in a copy of these Pages for each partnership of which you were a member, and for each business carried on by the partnership.

Partnership details

Partnership reference number

4.1

Partnership trade or profession

4.2

- Date you started being a partner (if during 1998-99)   **4.3**   /   /

- Date you stopped being a partner (if during 1998-99)   **4.4**   /   /

Your share of the partnership's trading or professional income

Basis period begins   **4.5**   /   /   and ends   **4.6**   /   /

- Your share of the profit or loss of this year's account for tax purposes   **4.7** £

- Adjustment to arrive at profit or loss for this basis period   **4.8** £

- Overlap profit brought forward   **4.9** £   Deduct overlap relief used this year   **4.10** £

- Overlap profit carried forward   **4.11** £

- Adjustment for farmers' averaging (see Notes, page PN3 if the partnership made a loss in 1998-99) or foreign tax deducted, if tax credit relief not claimed   **4.12** £

Net profit for 1998-99 (if loss, enter '0' in box 4.13 and enter the loss in box 4.14)   **4.13** £

Allowable loss for 1998-99   **4.14** £

- Loss offset against other income for 1998-99   **4.15** £

- Loss to carry back   **4.16** £

- Loss to carry forward (that is, allowable loss not claimed in any other way)   **4.17** £

- Losses brought forward from last year   **4.18** £

- Losses brought forward from last year used this year   **4.19** £

box 4.13 *minus* box 4.19

Taxable profit after losses brought forward   **4.20** £

- Add amounts **not** included in the partnership accounts that are needed to calculate your taxable profit (for example, Enterprise Allowance (Business Start-up Allowance) received in 1998-99)   **4.21**

box 4.20 + box 4.21

Total taxable profits from this business   **4.22** £

Class 4 National Insurance Contributions

- Tick this box if exception or deferment applies **4.23** ☐

- Adustments to profit chargeable to Class 4 National Insurance Contributions **4.24** £

Class 4 National Insurance Contributions due **4.25** £

Your share of taxed income

- Share of taxed income (liable at 20%) **4.70** £

Your share of Partnership Trading and Professional Profits

from box 4.22

- Share of partnership profits (other than that liable at 20%) **4.73** £

Your share of tax paid

- Share of Income Tax paid **4.74** £

- Share of SC60 deductions **4.75** £

- Share of tax deducted from trading income (not SC60 deductions) **4.75A** £

boxes 4.74 + 4.75 + 4.75A

4.77 £

Additional information

FILL THIS IN IF:	WHERE TO FIND THE INFORMATION	**What to enter**
You were entitled to a share of profits, losses or income from a business which you carried on in partnership. (See also boxes 4.1 to 4.22 on the previous page.)	You will have received a partnership statement for each partnership for which you were a partner and for each business if the partnership carried on more than one business.	You need to complete separate partnership pages for each statement. Some of the information requested is similar to that covered under the self-employed section (see page 36).

LAND AND PROPERTY

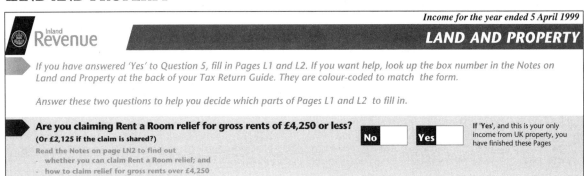

Income for the year ended 5 April 1999

LAND AND PROPERTY

If you have answered 'Yes' to Question 5, fill in Pages L1 and L2. If you want help, look up the box number in the Notes on Land and Property at the back of your Tax Return Guide. They are colour-coded to match the form.

Answer these two questions to help you decide which parts of Pages L1 and L2 to fill in.

Are you claiming Rent a Room relief for gross rents of £4,250 or less?
(Or £2,125 if the claim is shared?)
Read the Notes on page LN2 to find out
- whether you can claim Rent a Room relief; and
- how to claim relief for gross rents over £4,250

No ☐   Yes ☐

If 'Yes', and this is your only income from UK property, you have finished these Pages

FILL THIS IN IF:

You wish to claim Rent-a-Room relief and the gross rents are £4,250 or less a year. (If more see page 46.)

What to enter

Tick either the 'Yes' or 'No' box; if 'Yes' and you have no other income from land or property you need not complete the rest of this form.

Is your income from furnished holiday lettings?
If 'No', turn over and fill in Page L2 to give details of your property income

No ☐   Yes ☐

If 'Yes', fill in boxes 5.1 to 5.18 before completing Page L2

Furnished holiday lettings

- Income from furnished holiday lettings — **5.1** £

■ *Expenses* (furnished holiday lettings only)

- Rent, rates, insurance, ground rents etc. — **5.2** £
- Repairs, maintenance and renewals — **5.3** £
- Finance charges, including interest — **5.4** £
- Legal and professional costs — **5.5** £
- Cost of services provided, including wages — **5.6** £
- Other expenses — **5.7** £

total of boxes 5.2 to 5.7
5.8 £

box 5.1 *minus* box 5.8
Net profit (put figures in brackets if a loss) — **5.9** £

■ *Tax adjustments*

- Private use — **5.10** £
- Balancing charges — **5.11** £

box 5.10 + box 5.11
5.12 £

- Capital allowances — **5.13** £

boxes 5.9 + 5.12 *minus* box 5.13
Profit for the year (copy to box 5.19). If loss, enter '0' in box 5.14 and put the loss in box 5.15 — **5.14** £

	boxes 5.9 + 5.12 *minus* box 5.13
Loss for the year (if you have entered '0' in box 5.14)	**5.15** £
● Loss offset against 1998-99 total income	**5.16** £
	see Notes, page LN4
● Loss carried back	**5.17** £
	see Notes, page LN4
● Loss offset against other income from property (copy to box 5.38)	**5.18** £

WHERE TO FIND THE INFORMATION

Records of rent received and of expenses and bills paid.

FILL THIS IN IF:

You have income from furnished holiday lettings in the U.K. (tick the 'Yes' box).Note: the forms start on page 44. Any income from overseas should not be entered here but under the Foreign supplementary pages (see page 47).

What to enter

The relevant income and expenditure. See page 46 for the types of expenditure you can claim and see page 39 for capital allowance details.

Other property income

■ *Income*

	copy from box 5.14		Tax deducted	
● Furnished holiday lettings profits	**5.19** £			
● Rents and other income from land and property	**5.20** £		**5.21** £	
				boxes 5.19 + 5.20 + 5.22
● Chargeable premiums	**5.22** £			**5.23** £

■ *Expenses* (do not include figures you have already put in boxes 5.2 to 5.7 on Page L1)

● Rent, rates, insurance, ground rents etc.	**5.24** £	
● Repairs, maintenance and renewals	**5.25** £	
● Finance charges, including interest	**5.26** £	
● Legal and professional costs	**5.27** £	
● Costs of services provided, including wages	**5.28** £	
		total of boxes 5.24 to 5.29
● Other expenses	**5.29** £	**5.30** £

	box 5.23 *minus* box 5.30
Net profit (put figures in brackets if a loss)	**5.31** £

■ *Tax adjustments*

● Private use	**5.32** £	
		box 5.32 + box 5.33
● Balancing charges	**5.33** £	**5.34** £
● Rent a Room exempt amount	**5.35** £	
● Capital allowances	**5.36** £	
● 10% wear and tear	**5.37** £	
		total of boxes 5.35 to 5.38
● Furnished holiday lettings losses (from box 5.18)	**5.38** £	**5.39** £

		boxes 5.31 + 5.34 *minus* box 5.39	
Adjusted profit (if loss enter '0' in box 5.40 and put the loss in box 5.41)		**5.40** £	

	boxes 5.31 + 5.34 *minus* box 5.39	
Adjusted loss (if you have entered '0' in box 5.40)	**5.41** £	

● Loss brought forward from previous year **5.42** £

Profit for the year   box 5.40 *minus* box 5.42   **5.43** £

● Loss offset against total income **5.44** £

● Loss to carry forward to following year **5.45** £

● Pooled expenses from 'one estate election' carried forward **5.46** £

Tick box 5.47 if these Pages include details of property let jointly **5.47**

FILL THIS IN IF:

You have other property or Rent-a-Room income over £4,250 a year.

WHERE TO FIND THE INFORMATION

Records of rent received and records of expenses and bills paid.

What to enter

The relevant income and expenditure. See below for the types of expenditure you can claim, and see page 39 for capital allowances details.

REMEMBER:

Rent-a-Room scheme with income over £4,250 a year:

You have the option of either paying the excess without any deduction for allowable expenses, or calculating any profit made (gross rents less actual allowable expenses) and paying tax on that profit in the normal way.

An individual's £4,250 limit is halved if, at any time during a tax year, someone else received income from letting the same property.

JOINT NAMES

If a *husband and wife* own a property that is let, the tax office will assume that any income from this asset is divided equally.

You should enter in your tax return one half of the income and expenses, and tick box 5.47 to indicate to the tax office that it is a joint holding.

If the ownership is *not* held equally, then ask your tax office for Form 17 in which you can jointly declare the actual ownership split. Such declaration takes effect from the date it is made provided that the form is sent to your tax office within 60 days.

TAX TIP:

What expenses can you claim against property income?

Some, or all of the following should be considered:

Rent paid, and water rates

General maintenance and repairs of the property, garden and furniture and fittings

Costs of agents for letting, and collecting rents

Insurance

Interest payable on a loan to purchase, or improve investment property (but there are restrictions – see page 18)

Charges for preparing inventories

Legal fees – on renewing a tenancy agreement, for leases of not more than 50 years, or on the initial grant of a lease not exceeding 21 years

Accountancy fees to prepare and agree your income

Costs of collecting rents which could in some cases include your travelling expenses to and from the property

Costs of services e.g. porters, cleaners, security.

Wear and tear allowance for furniture and fittings; generally 10 per cent of the basic rent receivable. As an alternative, the cost of renewals may be claimed

Council tax.

FOREIGN

You will need these forms if you receive income, pensions, social security benefits, etc. from abroad.

Income and gains and tax credit relief for the year ended 5 April 1999

Inland Revenue

FOREIGN

If you have answered 'Yes' to Question 6, fill in these Pages. If you want help, look up the box number in the Notes on Foreign at the back of your Tax Return Guide. They are colour-coded to match the form.

Foreign savings

Fill in columns A to E, and tick the box in column E if you want to claim tax credit relief.

Country / tick box if income is unremittable / **A** ▼		Amount before tax / **B**	UK tax / **C**	Foreign tax / **D**	Amount chargeable / tick box to claim tax credit relief / **E** ▼	
■ *Dividends, interest, and other savings income* -see Notes, page FN4		£	£	£	£	
		£	£	£	£	
		£	£	£	£	

FILL THIS IN IF:	**WHERE TO FIND THE INFORMATION**
You receive income, pensions or benefits from abroad.	Overseas dividend vouchers, bank statements, overseas pension and social security benefit statements, foreign tax assessments and actual receipts for any foreign tax paid.

What to enter

These supplementary pages are divided into four sections. Only the first part of the form is reproduced above.

Boxes 6.1 and 6.2 cover income from foreign savings – fill in the figures in the appropriate columns.

Boxes 6.3 to 6.8 are for other overseas income, including pensions and social security benefits.

Boxes 6.9 and 6.10 enable you to reclaim any foreign tax paid.

Boxes 6.11 to 6.31 cover income from land and property abroad – the information required is similar to that for income from U.K. land and property (see page 44).

REMEMBER:

Keep details as to how you make up the figures for although you do not have to enter the names and addresses of the properties, pension providers, etc. on the form, the tax office may ask for them.

Capital gains should be shown on the Capital Gains pages (see page 49) not on these Foreign pages.

TRUSTS ETC.

You will need this form if you receive income from a trust, settlement or estate. Ring the Inland Revenue order line on 0645 000404 if you need a form.

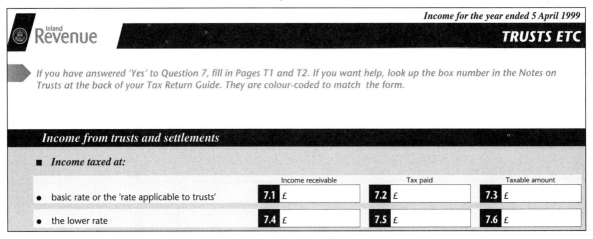

Inland Revenue

Income for the year ended 5 April 1999

TRUSTS ETC

If you have answered 'Yes' to Question 7, fill in Pages T1 and T2. If you want help, look up the box number in the Notes on Trusts at the back of your Tax Return Guide. They are colour-coded to match the form.

Income from trusts and settlements

■ *Income taxed at:*

	Income receivable	Tax paid	Taxable amount
● basic rate or the 'rate applicable to trusts'	7.1 £	7.2 £	7.3 £
● the lower rate	7.4 £	7.5 £	7.6 £

FILL THIS IN IF:	**WHERE TO FIND THE INFORMATION**	**What to enter**
You were entitled to receive income from a trust fund set up by someone else or you have received income from a discretionary or accumulation trust.	You should receive a statement or certificate from the Trustees – ask for one if you have not received it.	Fill in the boxes showing income received, tax paid and gross amount (i.e. taxable amount) differentiating between the various tax rates.

Income from the estates of deceased persons

■ *Income bearing:*

	Income receivable	Tax paid	Taxable amount
● basic rate tax	7.7 £	7.8 £	7.9 £
● lower rate tax	7.10 £	7.11 £	7.12 £
● non-repayable lower rate tax	7.13 £	7.14 £	7.15 £
● non-repayable basic rate tax	7.16 £	7.17 £	7.18 £
● Total foreign tax for which tax credit relief not claimed		7.19 £	

FILL THIS IN IF:	**WHERE TO FIND THE INFORMATION**	**What to enter**
You have received any payment from the estate of someone who has died.	The personal representative or solicitor should send you a statement giving details and a tax deduction certificate (a form RI85) showing the tax that has been deducted.	As with Trusts above, complete the boxes differentiating between the various tax rates.

CAPITAL GAINS

A capital gain is any profit arising when you sell, transfer, give, receive compensation for, or otherwise dispose of any of your assets or possessions.

Some assets are exempt from this tax (see page 50) but you will need to fill in these pages if you have made a capital profit (or loss) on assets that are taxable.

There is no capital gains tax payable on death but there may be an Inheritance Tax liability.

For the year ended 5 April 1999

Inland Revenue

CAPITAL GAINS

Name _____

Tax reference _____

Fill in these boxes first

If you want help, look up the box numbers in the Notes.

*Please complete Pages CG2 and CG3 **before** filling in the rest of this Page. If you think you will need more than one copy of Pages CG2 and CG3 make photocopies before you begin filling them in.*

Your 1998-99 Capital Gains Tax liability

- Total taxable gains from Page CG3 overleaf — **8.7** £ _____

- Your taxable gains *minus* the annual exempt amount — **8.8** £ _____ *(box 8.7 minus £6,800)*

- Additional liability in respect of non-resident or dual resident trusts — **8.9** £ _____

Capital losses

(Remember if your loss arose on a transaction with a connected person, see Notes page CGN11, you can only set that loss against gains you make on disposals to that same connected person)

This year's losses

- Total from Page CG2 — **8.10** £ _____

- Used against gains — **8.11** £ _____

- Used against earlier years' gains (see Notes, page CGN8) — **8.12** £ _____

- Used against income (see Notes, page CGN7)
  - **8.13A** £ _____ amount claimed against income of 1998-99
  - **8.13B** £ _____ amount claimed against income of 1997-98
  - **8.13** £ _____ *(box 8.13A + box 8.13B)*

- This year's unused losses — **8.14** £ _____ *(box 8.10 minus (boxes 8.11+ 8.12+ 8.13))*

Earlier years' losses

- Unused losses of 1996-97 and 1997-98 — **8.15** £ _____

- Used this year (losses from box 8.15 are used in priority to losses from box 8.18) — **8.16** £ _____

- Remaining unused losses of 1996-97 and 1997-98 — **8.17** £ _____ *(box 8.15 minus box 8.16)*

- Unused losses of 1995-96 and earlier years | **8.18** £

	box 8.6 *minus* box 8.16
	8.19 £

- Used this year (losses from box 8.15 are used in priority to losses from box 8.18)

◼ *Total of unused losses to carry forward*

	box 8.14 + box 8.17
	8.20 £

- Carried forward losses of 1996-97 and later years

	box 8.18 *minus* box 8.19
	8.21 £

- Carried forward losses of 1995-96 and earlier years

FILL THIS IN IF:

You sold or gave away assets to the value of £13,600 or more and your chargeable gains for tax purposes were £6,800 or more in the year ended 5 April 1999. (See also boxes on previous page.)

WHERE TO FIND THE INFORMATION

You will need copies of contract notes for the sale or purchase of shares; invoices and letters about the purchase or sale of other assets, and invoices for allowable expenses which you can claim.

What to enter

You will certainly need supplementary sheets to list details as to how you make up the figures that you put in the boxes, and the summary sheet on pages 2 and 3 of the capital gains pages (not reproduced above).

The first part of the return deals with chargeable gains and allowable losses and the second part enables you to keep an ongoing record of capital losses.

REMEMBER:

There is relief for inflation – a combination of an indexation allowance and tapering relief. A higher rate of relief is available for business assets The percentages and formulae used will be detailed in the notes that come from your tax office with this form.

Assets which are free from Capital Gains Tax

Private motor cars.

A house owned and occupied by you which is your main residence.

Chattels – such as jewellery, pictures and furniture – where the proceeds are £6,000 or less, with marginal relief up to £15,000.

Life policies and deferred annuities (unless sold on by original owner).

National Savings Certificates; Premium Bonds.

Shares subscribed for under the BES and EIS.

Shares subscribed for in approved quoted Venture Capital Trusts.

Personal Equity Plan (PEP) investments held for at least a full calendar year, starting 1 January; also transfers of all-employee share schemes to a single company PEP.

Save As You Earn schemes.

TESSA accounts.

Government stocks and public corporation stocks guaranteed by the Government.

Qualifying corporate bonds.

Gambling, pools and lottery winnings and prizes.

Decorations for gallantry, unless purchased.

Compensation for damages.

Gifts of assets to a charity.

Gifts of outstanding public interest given to the nation.

Land and buildings given to the National Trust

Gains up to a certain amount on the sale of your business if you are 50 or over, or retiring earlier due to ill health (phased out from 6.4.99).

Foreign currency for personal use.

NON-RESIDENCE, ETC.

Whether you are resident or domiciled in the U.K. or abroad can affect your liability to Income Tax or Capital Gains Tax.

For the year ended 5 April 1999

Inland **Revenue**

NON-RESIDENCE ETC.

If you have answered 'Yes' to Question 9, fill in Pages NR1 and NR2. If you want help, look up the box number in the Notes on Non-residence etc. at the back of your Tax Return Guide. They are colour-coded to match the form.

Residence status

I am *(please tick appropriate box)*

- resident in the UK **9.1**
- not resident in the UK **9.2**
- ordinarily resident in the UK **9.3**
- not ordinarily resident in the UK **9.4**
- not domiciled in the UK (and it is relevant to my Income Tax or Capital Gains Tax liability) **9.5**
- claiming split-year treatment **9.6**
- claiming personal allowances as a non-resident **9.7**
- resident in a country other than the UK (under a double taxation agreement) at the same time as being resident in the UK **9.8**

Information required if you claim to be non-resident in the UK for the whole of 1998-99

- Are you in any of the following categories:

  - a Commonwealth citizen (this includes a British citizen) or an EEA national?

  - a present or former employee of the British Crown (including a civil servant, member of the armed forces etc)?

  - a UK missionary society employee?

  - a civil servant in a territory under the protection of the British Crown?

  - a resident of the Isle of Man or the Channel Islands?

  - a former resident of the UK and you live abroad for the sake of your own health or the health of a member of your family who lives with you?

  - a widow or widower of an employee of the British Crown?

  Yes **9.9**   No **9.10**

- How many days have you spent in the UK, excluding days of arrival and departure, during the year ended 5 April 1999? *Enter the number of days* **9.11** *days*

FILL THIS IN IF:

You know that you are non-resident or domiciled in the U.K. for tax purposes, or if you have moved abroad or have been living abroad, for this may affect your tax status and tax liabilities (only the first part of the form is reproduced here).

TAX TIP:

The rules governing the legal status of a person and the tax implications are amongst some of the most difficult tax legislation, and it is wise to get a tax adviser to handle these matters for you.

What to enter

These supplementary pages contain a sequence of 'Yes'/'No' questions so that the tax office can establish your status for tax purposes.

PAYE Coding Notice

The tax office gives employers a PAYE code for each of their employees. This code is made up from the information your tax office have on their files either as a result of information that they have found out or from a tax return form sent in by you. The tax office send you a Coding Notice similar to that shown below which you need to check. If it is wrong you will pay the incorrect amount of tax. Your employers are told only the code (not the full details) so that they can calculate how much of your pay is tax free.

Inland Revenue

PAYE Coding Notice

This form shows your tax code for the tax year

> *Please keep all your coding notices. You may need to refer to them if you have to fill in a Tax Return.*

Tax Office telephone ☎	Date of issue

Please quote your Tax reference and National Insurance number if you contact us

Tax reference	National Insurance number

Your tax code for the year shown above is

This tax code is used to deduct tax payable on your income from

If you move to another job, your new employer will normally continue to use this tax code.
The tax code is made up as follows:

See note	Your tax allowances	£
	Total allowances	

The left-hand side shows your allowances, allowable expenses, and any claim for higher rate tax relief on allowable payments on which basic rate tax has been deducted (e.g. a personal pension payment, or Gift Aid to charity). Payments to personal pension plans and free-standing additional voluntary contribution schemes will also be shown here.
There may also be a note of Estimated Total Income to be used in calculating your age allowance restriction.

Your tax free amount for the year is £   , making your Tax Code

*The **Tax free amount** is the difference between your **Total allowances** and **Total deductions**.*

See example overleaf

The right-hand side shows any taxable State Pension or benefits you have received e.g. a company car, fuel, medical insurance.

Other emoluments could refer to casual earnings, after expenses, declared by you on your tax return (or an estimate made by the tax office).

Allowance restrictions refer to the married, additional personal or widow's bereavement allowances, mortgage payments not under MIRAS or most maintenance payments. The full amount of these allowances is shown on the left-hand side, but you are allowed relief at only 15 per cent for 1998-99 and only 10 per cent for 1999-2000 so part of it has to be 'clawed back'.

These 'clawback' figures will normally be:

	1998-99 £	1999-2000 £
Lower rate	457	950
Basic rate	660	1070
Higher rate	1187	1420

but the figures may vary, for example, if you get the age allowance.

Any untaxed interest will be stated here. Any under or over payment of tax refers to a notice of assessment for a previous year.

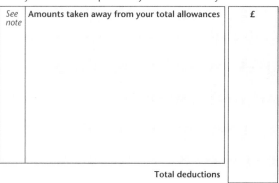

The 'See note' columns below refer to the numbered notes in the guidance leaflet P3 *Understanding Your Tax Code*. Leaflet P3 also tells you about the **letter part** of your tax code.

Check that the details are correct. If you think they are wrong, or you have any queries, contact your Tax Office (details above).

This coding notice replaces any previous notice for the year. You should pass it to your tax adviser if you have one.

See note	Amounts taken away from your total allowances	£
	Total deductions	

TAX TIP:

If your coding notice is wrong write to the tax office, or if you haven't filled in a tax return for a year or two then ask for a tax return and fill it in.

Your code is found by deducting the total of the left-hand side from the right-hand side and omitting the last figure. The higher your code, the lower your tax.

The letter shown after your code defines your status (e.g. L – basic personal allowance entitlement; H – personal allowance plus married couple's allowance or additional person allowance at basic rate [P is for lower rate and A for higher rate]; P – single pensioner; V – married pensioner). Letter T is used if there are items that need reviewing or if you have asked for other codes not to be used e.g. you don't want your employer to know your personal circumstances. OT means that no allowances have been given – this is often used if you haven't sent in a tax return for a long time.

Other codes are: NT – no tax payable; BR – all earnings to be taxed at the basic rate; DO – to be taxed at the higher rate.

K codes are negative codes, used where taxpayer's benefits in kind, and other taxable income not taxed at source, exceed their total allowances.

How to work out your own tax liability (or tax repayment)

The tax system in the U.K. is unnecessarily complicated, so it is very difficult to produce an overall grid to cover all contingencies.

However, this **Quick Tax Check** should be suitable for most people.

The grid is designed for the tax year ended 5 April 1999, but you could use it for earlier years provided that you alter the tax rates accordingly. Refer to the first section of this book, showing you how to fill in a tax return, to provide you with definitions of the wording used.

Do not include any income that is tax free (e.g. PEPs, TESSAs, the first £70 interest on National Savings Ordinary accounts, National Savings Certificate interest).

Your income	Tax deducted	Gross amount
Salary or wages, including any profit sharing schemes Show the amount after deducting any pension scheme contribution, payroll giving, or tax-free profit-related pay	....	....
State pension		....
Other pensions	....	....
Benefits from employer (e.g. company car)		....
Taxable profits from self-employment or freelance earnings etc. after capital allowances and loss relief		....
Casual earnings, after expenses		....
Interest received	....	....
Dividends received (you should add the tax credit to this and then show it separately in the tax deducted column)	....	....
Social security benefits that are taxable		....
Income from land and property (taxable amounts only)		....
Any other income	....	....
	£ a	£ A

Less: Allowable Expenses

	Tax deducted	Gross amount
Personal pension contributions including retirement annuity contributions for this year (exclude any carry back to previous years)	....	....
Vocational training payments	....	....
Charitable covenant or gift aid	....	....
Maintenance payments (old contract) – excess over £1,900	....	....
Interest paid on qualifying loans, other than your own home	....	....
Other expenses allowed for tax	....	....
Total allowable expenses	£ b	£ B
Tax paid and 'Net income'	£a – b = T	£A – B = C

Less: Your claim for:
Personal allowance ....
    (but deduct any Income limit reduction if over 65 –
    see table on page 72) ....
Blind person's allowance ....

                      £ D

<u>Income on which tax is payable</u>   £C – D = E

<u>Tax payable</u> (see band limits on page 72)
    £   at 20% ....
    £   *at 20% on savings income ....
    £   at 23% ....
    £   at 40% ....

    £ E   £ F

Less: Your claim for personal allowances that are
available at only 15% (10% for 1999-2000)
    Married couple's allowance ....
    Additional personal allowance ....
    Widow's bereavement allowance ....
    Maintenance or alimony (maximum £1,900) ....

               £ G

          at 15%   = £ H

              £F – H = I

Less: Enterprise Investment Scheme or
    Venture Capital Trust shares £   at 20% ....

                  J

Less: **Tax already paid** (see page 54)   T

Tax due: (if J is higher than T) or   }
Tax reclaimed (if T is higher than J)   £ K

*Savings income is treated as the highest part of your income. Any savings income which would be taxed at 23% is taxed at 20% instead, so that after the tax credit or tax deducted in T you have no liability on it.

    Example: Taxable income £28,000 1998–99 includes £6,000 from savings income.

    £ 4,300 at 20%
    £22,800 at 23% becomes {   £17,700 at 23%
    £ 900 at 40%   £ 5,100 at 20%

Tax Repayments

At the end of each tax year on 5 April you should check to see exactly what income you received during the year and what tax you have actually paid. Use the Quick Tax Check on page 54.

If you have paid too much you can get a repayment of tax.

To reclaim tax ask your tax office for leaflet IR110 which includes a form R95 'Request for repayment claim form'. You will be sent a Form R40. Complete it in the same way as a tax return and send the form to your tax office.

Where most of your income has already had tax deducted before you receive it (for example dividends), you may be able to make quarterly, half-yearly or annual repayment claims.

Is interest being deducted from your savings?

If your total income from all sources for the year does not exceed your allowances and you have any interest from banks, building societies or local authorities, you should register to have such interest paid to you without tax being deducted.

Ask your bank, building society or local authority for Form R85, complete it and return it to the branch that holds your account; or ask any tax office for booklet IR110 – this has lots of helpful advice as well as a form R85 and a repayment claim form, R40.

Inland Revenue

Registration form for Interest without tax taken off

Use this form only if the person entitled to the interest usually lives in the UK.
Read the notes below and on the back of this form to find out if you can register. If you can register, complete the form **in full using black ink.**
If the form is for somebody else please complete it with **their** details.
Complete a form for each account on which you expect to receive interest.
If your interest is paid by a local authority please read "bank or building society" as including a reference to "local authority".

For official use only
Date of receipt

	Initials	Surname
Name		

Permanent address
The address you give should be that of the place where you usually live. **See note overleaf on 'Permanent address'**

Postcode

	Day	Month	Year
Date of birth			

Has the person named above worked in the UK in the last 3 years ?
For the form to be valid please "√" either 'Yes' or 'No'   Yes   No

If "yes" and the person named above is 16 or over enter
National Insurance number here (*see note overleaf*)

Name of bank or building society

Branch

Account number *Please quote the number in full*

Is this a **joint account**?   *Please '√'*   Yes   No   If " Yes " each person able to register must complete a separate form.

I certify that
• the information given above is correct;

It is a serious offence to make a false declaration.

Details of employee leaving work (Form P45)

When you leave an employment, your employer must give you a P45 form. You will get three parts: Part 1A you keep yourself as a record of your earnings and tax paid, etc.

Parts 2 and 3 you give to your new employers if you start another job. Your new employers will keep part 2, and will complete part 3 and send it to their tax office so that your tax file can be kept up to date and the tax inspector is aware of your movements.

Inland Revenue

Details of employee leaving work **P45**
Copy for employee ★ **Part 1A**

1 PAYE Reference

District number   Reference number

2 Employee's National Insurance number

(Mr Mrs Miss Ms)

3 Surname

First name(s)

4 Leaving date   Day   Month   Year   19

5 Tax Code at leaving date. *'X' in the box means Week 1 or Month 1 basis applies*   Code   Week 1 or Month 1

6 Last entries on *Deductions Working Sheet* (P11) *If there is an 'X' at item 5, there will be no entries here*

Week or month number   Week   Month

Total pay to date   £   p

Total tax to date   £   p

7 This employment pay and tax. *If no entry here, the amounts are those shown at item 6*

Total pay in this employment   £   p

Total tax in this employment   £   p

What to do with the form P45

If you have ceased work permanently

Send the form to your tax office whose district is stamped on the form. Also write a letter confirming that you have either retired, ceased working or have become self-employed and ask for a claim form for any tax repayment due.

If you have ceased work temporarily

When you change employment or are made redundant, and there is a gap between one job and the next, send in your form P45 as above, stating that you are temporarily unemployed. Alternatively, if you are claiming the jobseeker's allowance, hand your P45 to your Social Security Office who will advise you on the proportion of any benefit that is taxable. Normally any adjustments to your tax liability will be made when you start a new employment in the current tax year.

If you do not start a job by the following 5 April, check your total income and tax to see if there is a repayment or underpayment of tax due (use the Quick Guide on page 54).

Certificate of Pay, Income Tax and NIC (Form P60)

Your employer has by law to give you a P60 form by 31 May after the end of every tax year. It may have slight variation in design, but it has to contain the following information:

Your National Insurance number. →

The amounts paid by you and your employer in National Insurance contributions. →

These boxes will have totals for the pay you have received from the employer who has issued you with this form together with the amount of tax deducted. There will also be totals for pay and tax in respect of previous employers for whom you worked in this tax year. →

Do not destroy　　　　　　　　　　　　　　　　　**P60** C

Employer's name and address

Tax Office name

For employer's use

Employee's details　　　　　　　　　　　　　　　　Sex

National Insurance number

"M" if Male, "F" if Female

Surname

First two forenames

Works/payroll no. etc

National Insurance contributions in this employment

NI contribution table letter	Earnings on which employee's contributions payable (whole £s only)	Total of employee's and employer's contributions payable	Employee's contributions payable
	1a　　£	1b　　£　p	1c　　£　p

Pay and Income Tax details　　　　　　　　　　　　**Pay**

£　p

Employee's Widows & Orphans/ Life Assurance contributions in this employment
£　p

In previous employment(s)

In this employment

Figures shown here should be used for your tax return, if you get one

Total for year

Final tax code

Employer: *This form P60 can be machine-completed by desk-top laser printer or other suitable sheet-feed printer. Forms*

Indicates a deduction for this insurance.

Your tax code at the year end.

REMEMBER:

What to do with the form P60:
Keep it as a record of your earnings for the tax year and the amount of tax deducted.

Use it to fill in your tax return.

Use it as additional proof of income if you arrange a mortgage or a loan.

Use it to check any tax assessment that is sent to you,

---

60 Certificate of Pay, Income Tax and National Insurance contributions

Tax Office number and Reference

/

Tax Year to 5 April

Employee's private address

Male, emale

If you change your address, please let your Tax Office and the Contributions Agency know

To the employee:
Please keep this certificate in a safe place as you will not be able to get a duplicate. **You will need it if you have to fill in a Tax Return.**
You can also use it to check that your employer is deducting the right type of National Insurance contributions for you and using your correct National Insurance number. If this is not the case, please tell your employer.
By law you are required to tell the Tax Office of any income that is not fully taxed, even if you are not sent a Tax Return. *INLAND REVENUE*

Earnings on which employee's conts. at Contracted-out rate payable incl. in 1a (whole £s only)	Employee's contributions at Contracted-out rate included in 1c	Scheme Contracted-out number (For Contracted-out Money Purchase Schemes only)
1d £	**1e** £ p	S
		S
		S
		S

Tax deducted

p

£ p

If net refund enter "R" in this box

From Employer/Paying Office:
This certificate shows the total amount of pay for Income Tax purposes that I/we have paid to you in the year. Any overtime, bonus, commission etc, statutory sick pay or statutory maternity pay is included. It also gives details of the total Income Tax and National Insurance contributions deducted by me/us (less any refunds).

Week 53 payment indicator

Forms P14 (DSS and Inland Revenue copies) are on separate sheets 1 and 2. **P60**(Laser-Sheet 3)

Your tax reference number and the tax year to which the form relates.

Reference number of contracted-out money purchase pension scheme.

Sometimes the PAYE year has 53 weeks instead of 52. (This box is for the convenience of the tax office.)

FINANCIAL TIP:

If you want to check whether your contributions are up to date to ensure you can claim full social security pension benefits, or to obtain an estimate of your state retirement pension, write to The Benefits Agency, RPFA, at DSS Longbenton, Benton Park Road, Newcastle upon Tyne, NE98 1YX.

Return of expenses and benefits (Form P11D)

The form reproduced below is completed annually by an employer for all staff who receive earnings, expenses and benefits which total £8,500 a year or more, and for all directors. It shows all perks, benefits and expenses that were paid or given by your employer. Your employers should give you a copy of this form, which they will have sent to the tax office by 6 July, as you need to know what figures to put in your tax return. You also need to have the figures so that you can check any tax assessment sent to you and to check your PAYE code.

Inland Revenue

P11D EXPENSES AND BENEFITS 1998-99

Note to employer
Complete this return for a director, or an employee who earned at a rate of £8,500 a year or more during the year 6 April 1998 to 5 April 1999. Do not include expenses and benefits covered by a dispensation or PAYE settlement agreement. Read the P11D Guide and booklet 480, Chapter 24, before you complete the form. Send the completed P11D and form P11D(b) to the Tax Office by 6 July 1999. You must give a copy of this information to the director or employee by the same date. The term employee is used to cover both directors and employees throughout the rest of this form.

Note to employee
Your employer has filled in this form. Keep it in a safe place as you may not be able to get a duplicate. You will need it for your tax records and to complete your 1998-99 Tax Return if you get one. Your tax code may need to be adjusted to take account of the information given on this P11D. The box numbers on this P11D have the same numbering as the Employment Pages of the Tax Return, for example, 1.12. Include the total figures in the corresponding box on the Tax Return, unless you think some other figure is more appropriate.

Employer's details
Employer's name

PAYE tax reference

Employee's details
Employee's name

Tick here if a director

Works number or department

National Insurance number

A	• Assets transferred (cars, property, goods or other assets)			
		Cost/ Market value	Amount made good or from which tax deducted	Cash equivalent
	Description of asset	£	− £	= **1.12** £

B	• Payments made on behalf of employee	
	Description of payment	**1.12** £
	Tax on notional payments not borne by employee within 30 days of receipt of each notional payment	**1.12** £

C	• Vouchers or credit cards			
		Gross amount	Amount made good or from which tax deducted	Cash equivalent
	Value of vouchers and payments made using credit cards or tokens	£	− £	= **1.13** £

D	• Living accommmodation	
		Cash equivalent
	Cash equivalent of accommodation provided for employee, or his/ her family or household	**1.14** £

E	• Mileage allowance			
		Gross amount	Amount made good or from which tax deducted	Taxable payment
	Car and mileage allowances paid for employee's car	£	− £	= **1.15** £

F • **Cars and car fuel**
If more than two cars were made available, either at the same time or in succession, please give details on a separate sheet

	Car 1	Car 2
Make and Model		
Dates first registered	/ /	/ /

Dates car was available — From / / To / / | From / / To / /

Business mileage used in calculation for this car. *Tick only one box for each car.* *If the car was not available for part of the year, the business mileage limits are reduced proportionately.*

Car 1: 2,499 or less ☐ 2,500 to 17,999 ☐ 18,000 or more ☐
Car 2: 2,499 or less ☐ 2,500 to 17,999 ☐ 18,000 or more ☐

Enter engine size and tick type of fuel only if there is a car fuel scale charge
Car 1: Engine size in cc ___ cc Petrol ☐ Diesel ☐
Car 2: Engine size in cc ___ cc Petrol ☐ Diesel ☐

	Car 1	Car 2
List price of car *If there is no list price, or if it is a classic car, employers see booklet 480; employees see leaflet IR133*	£	£
Price of optional accessories fitted when car was first made available to the employee	£	£
Price of accessories added after the car was first made available to the employee	£	£
Capital contributions (maximum £5,000) the employee made towards the cost of car or accessories	£	£
Amount paid by employee for private use of the car	£	£
Cash equivalent of each car	£	£
Total cash equivalent of all cars available in 1998-99		**1.16** £
Cash equivalent of fuel for each car	£	£
Total cash equivalent of fuel for all cars available in 1998-99		**1.17** £

Car benefit

The annual tax benefit is calculated at 35% of the manufacturer's list price when new (less any personal contributions up to £5,000) – and includes delivery charges, VAT and any accessories over £100 added to the vehicle, unless they were for disabled persons. There are different valuations for classic cars and the list price is capped at £80,000.

You get a reduction of one-third of the benefit if your business mileage is between 2,500 and 17,999 miles a year and two-thirds if it is 18,000 a year or more. This net benefit (car benefit less any business mileage reduction) is reduced by a further one third for cars aged 4 years old or more at the end of the tax year.

Fuel benefit

If your employer provides fuel for your private motoring and you do not reimburse the full cost, you will be taxed on this benefit. (see table below).

Mileage allowance

If employers pay a mileage allowance to employees who use their own car for business, then any payment in excess of the official tax-free mileage rates will be taxable. (see table below).

Mileage Allowance	Up to 4,000 miles	Over 4,000 miles
Cars up to:		
1,000cc	28p	17p
1,001–1,500cc	35p	20p
1,501–2,000cc	45p	25p
over 2,000cc	63p	36p

The rates are the same for 1998–9 and 1999–2000.

Private fuel benefit	1999–2000 Petrol £	Diesel £	1998–99 Petrol £	Diesel £
1,400cc or less	1,210	1,540	1,010	1,280
1,401cc to 2,000cc	1,540	1,540	1,280	1,280
Over 2,000cc	2,270	2,270	1,890	1,890

There is no reduction for high business mileage.

G

- **Vans**

Cash equivalent of all vans made available for private use   **1.18** £

H

- **Interest-free and low interest loans**

If the total amount outstanding on all loans does not exceed £5,000 at any time in the year, there is no need for details in this section.

	Loan 1	Loan 2
Purpose of loan(s) – *please use the code shown in P11D Guide for employers*		
Number of joint borrowers *(if applicable)*		
Tick the box if the loan is within MIRAS		
Amount outstanding at 5 April 1998 or at date loan was made if later	£	£
Amount outstanding at 5 April 1999 or at date loan was discharged if earlier	£	£
Maximum amount outstanding at any time in the year	£	£
Total amount of interest paid by the borrower in 1998 - 99 – *enter "NIL" if none was paid*	£	£
Date loan was made or discharged in 1998 - 99 if applicable	/ /	/ /
Cash equivalent of loans after deducting any interest paid by the borrower	**1.19** £	**1.19** £

I

- **Mobile telephones**

Cash equivalent of mobile telephones provided   **1.20** £

J

- **Private medical treatment or insurance**

	Cost to you	Amount made good or from which tax deducted	Cash equivalent
Private medical treatment or insurance	£	− £	= **1.21** £

K

- **Qualifying relocation expenses payments and benefits (non-qualifying expenses go in P below)**

Excess over £8,000 of all qualifying relocation expenses payments and benefits for each move   **1.22** £

L

- **Services supplied**

	Cost to you	Amount made good or from which tax deducted	Cash equivalent
Services supplied to the employee	£	− £	= **1.22** £

M

- **Assets placed at the employee's disposal**

Description of asset	Annual value plus expenses incurred	Amount made good or from which tax deducted	Cash equivalent
	£	− £	= **1.22** £

N

- **Shares**

Tick the box if during the year there have been share-related benefits for the employee ☐

O

- **Other items**

	Cost to you	Amount made good or from which tax deducted	Cash equivalent
Subscriptions and professional fees	£	− £	= **1.22** £
Description of other items	£	− £	= **1.22** £

		Tax paid
Income tax paid but not deducted from director's remuneration		**1.22** £

P

- **Expenses payments made to, or on behalf of, the employee**

	Cost to you	Amount made good or from which tax deducted	Taxable payment
Travelling and subsistence payments	£	− £	= **1.23** £
Entertainment *(trading organisations read P11D Guide and then enter a tick or a cross as appropriate here)* ☐	£	− £	= **1.23** £
General expenses allowance for business travel	£	− £	= **1.23** £
Payments for use of home telephone	£	− £	= **1.23** £
Non-qualifying relocation expenses *(those not shown in section K)*	£	− £	= **1.23** £
Description of other expenses	£	− £	= **1.23** £

Is your benefit taxable?

Benefit	Employees earning £8,500 a year or more and directors	Employees earning less than £8,500 a year
Assets provided for your use free of charge (e.g. video)	Taxable at 20% of initial market value	Usually tax free
Canteen facilities available to directors and staff	Not taxable	Not taxable
Cash vouchers	Taxable	Taxable
Child care facilities (if qualifying conditions met)	Not taxable	Not taxable
Clothing and other goods given to you by your employer	Taxable	Taxed on second-hand value
Company cars, vans, etc.	Taxable at varying rates	Not taxable
Credit cards (for personal not business expenditure)	Taxable	Taxable
Exam prizes	Not taxable if reasonable and not part of employment contract	
Fuel for private use	Taxable at scale rate	Not taxable
Holidays	Taxable apart from business element	If employer pays directly, tax free
Interest-free loan	Normally taxable	Not taxable
In-house benefits	Taxable only on the value of the marginal or additional cost to the employer	
Jobfinder's grant	Not taxable	Not taxable
Living accommodation	Normally taxable at annual value unless essential for your employement	
Luncheon vouchers	Tax free up to 15p per working day.	
Mobile telephones (if used for private calls)	Taxable on £200	Not taxable
Outplacement counselling	Not taxable	Not taxable
Pension contributions and death in service cover	Normally tax free	
Private health schemes	Taxable	Not taxable
Prizes and incentive awards	Taxable	Taxable
Relocation expenses	Tax free up to £8,000	
Scholarships provided by employers' trust	Taxable	Not taxable
Season tickets for travel paid directly by employer	Taxable	Taxable
Share incentive schemes approved by tax inspector	Not taxable	Not taxable
Sick pay schemes	Taxable	Taxable
Workplace sports facilities	Not taxable	Not taxable

Self Assessment – How to calculate your own tax

If you want to calculate your tax when you send in your tax return, then you need to tick the appropriate 'Yes' box in Q18 on page 7 of your tax return (page 25 in this book).

You will need to fill in the Tax Calculation Working Sheets provided by your tax office with your tax return (telephone 0645 000404 if you haven't been sent one – they will send a set of sheets plus a guide booklet).

All the boxes are numbered according to the boxes in the main tax return and any supplementary pages that you need to complete, and although these forms look very complicated it is really a question of transferring all the figures into the correct summary boxes and following the instructions to ensure that you do the additions and subtractions according to the sequence.

The tax calculation working sheet reproduced here is the standard one with a prefix W before each box number; this will apply to the majority of taxpayers.

To complicate matters, you will need a different set of sheets if you have chargeable gains, or have received compensation payments, or AVC refunds, but these are mentioned specifically in the tax notes that come with your tax return.

REMEMBER:

You only have to fill in these tax calculation working sheets if you want to calculate your own tax – otherwise your tax office will calculate your tax and send you a demand.

The four pages of tax calculation working sheets contained in the Tax Calculation Guide sent to you with your tax return are reproduced overleaf, giving you the opportunity to keep your own permanent record.

Tax Calculation Working Sheet

Calculating your tax bill

▸ **Total income from:** *(copy figures from your Tax Return)*

- *Employment* including benefits and *minus* expenses for **each** employment

  Add income in:
  - boxes 1.8 to 1.10, **and**
  - boxes 1.12 to 1.23, **and**
  - boxes 1.27 and 1.28

  Deduct any figures in boxes 1.31 to 1.38

  Total taxable income

	First employment	Other employments
	£	£
	£	£
	£	+ £

If any of the sums on this page result in a negative amount, enter a zero in the appropriate box

W1 £

- *Share schemes* (from box 2.31) — **W2** £
- *Self-employment* (from box 3.88) — **W3** £
- *Partnerships* (from boxes 4.35, 4.70 and 4.73) — **W4** £
- *UK land and property* (from box 5.43) — **W5** £
- *Foreign income* (from boxes 6.2, 6.4 and 6.5) — **W6** £
- *Trusts, settlements or estates of deceased persons* (add together any figures in the 'right hand' column of the Trusts etc. Pages and deduct any figure in box 7.19) — **W7** £
- *UK savings and investments* (total any figures in the 'right hand' column on page 3 of your Tax Return) — **W8** £
- *UK pensions, retirement annuities and benefits* (add together any figures in the 'right hand' column of Question 11 on page 4 of your Tax Return *minus* any deduction in box 11.13) — **W9** £
- *Maintenance or alimony received* (from box 12.3) — **W10** £
- *Other income* (copy the figure in box 13.3 *minus* any figure in box 13.5) — **W11** £

Total income
total boxes W1 to W11
W12 £

Deductions for

- *Personal pension* (add together any figures in boxes 14.5, 14.10, 14.15, 14.16 and 14.17) — **W13** £
- *Vocational training* (multiply any figure in box 15.1 by $^{100}/_{77}$) — **W14** £
- *Interest on qualifying loans* (from box 15.3) — **W15** £
- *Maintenance or alimony paid* (see the notes on page 2 of this Guide) — **W16** £
- *Charitable covenants, annuities, Gift Aid and Millennium Gift Aid payments* (multiply any figures in boxes 15.9 and 15.10 by $^{100}/_{77}$) — **W17** £
- *Losses and post-cessation expenses* (from boxes 3.81, 4.15, 4.61, 5.16, 5.44, 8.13A and 15.11) — **W18** £
- *Trade union and friendly society death benefit payments* (from box 15.12) — **W19** £

Total deductions
total boxes W13 to W19
W20 £

box W12 *minus* box W20
Total income minus deductions **W21** £

Tax Calculation Working Sheet

Calculating your tax bill - continued

Reliefs
- you get basic rate relief automatically - further relief will be due if you are liable to higher rate tax.

from box W21

W22 £

If any of the sums on this page result in a negative amount, enter a zero in the appropriate box

- **Pension payments** (from boxes 14.15 and 14.17) — W23.1 £

- **Vocational training** (from box W14) — W23.2 £

box W23.1 + box W23.2
W23 £

box W22 + box W23
W24 £

Allowances given as a deduction from your income
- you may need to check your entitlement - see notes starting on page 3 of this Guide.

- **Personal allowance** - normally £4,195 unless you are non-resident and not claiming allowances — W25.1 £
+
- **Age-related personal allowance** - see notes page 3 — W25.2 £
+
- **Blind person's allowance** - enter £1,330 — W25.3 £
+
- **Transitional allowance** (from box 16.4) — W25.4 £
+
- **Blind person's surplus allowance from your spouse** (from box 16.27) — W25.5 £

total boxes W25.1 to W25.5
W25 £

If the figure in box W26 is £4,300 or less, do not fill in boxes W28 to W38

box W24 minus box W25
W26 £

box W26 x 20%
W27 £

Savings income taxable at the lower (20%) rate

- **Partnership savings** (from boxes 4.35 and 4.70) — W28.1 £
+
- **UK savings** (from box W8) — W28.2 £
+
- **Foreign savings** (from box 6.2) — W28.3 £
+
- **Trusts, settlements and estate income** (from boxes 7.6, 7.12 and 7.15) — W28.4 £

total boxes W28.1 to W28.4
W28 £

box W26 minus box W28
W29 £

W30 £ *4,300*

box W29 minus box W30
W31 £

box W31 x 3%
W32 £

If the figure in box W33 is £27,100 or less, do not fill in boxes W35 to W38

box W26 minus box W23 minus box 12.9
W33 £

W34 £ *27,100*

box W33 minus box W34
W35 £

box W35 x 17%
W36 £

lower of box W28 or box W35
W37 £

box W37 x 3%
W38 £

boxes W27 + W32 + W36 + W38

Income Tax due W39 £

Tax Calculation Working Sheet

Calculating your tax bill - continued

If any of the sums on this page result in a negative amount, enter a zero in the appropriate box

from page 6

W39 £

- **Venture Capital Trust and Enterprise Investment Scheme subscriptions**

box 15.7 + box 15.8

W40 £

box W40 x 20%

W41 £

box 15.2 x 10%

W42 £

Allowances and reliefs given in terms of tax
- these reduce your tax bill - you may need to use the Question 16 notes on pages 23 to 26 of the Tax Return Guide and starting on page 4 of this Guide.

- **Married couple's allowance**
  - see notes on pages 4 and 9 of this Guide

W43.1 £

+

- **Married couple's surplus allowance** (from box 16.28)

W43.2 £

+

- **Additional personal allowance**
  - usually £1,900, may be split with another person - see the notes

W43.3 £

+

- **Widow's bereavement allowance - £1,900** (if your husband died in 1997-98 or 1998-99 and you have not remarried)

W43.4 £

+

- **Maintenance and alimony** (boxes 15.4 and 15.5 - see the notes for box W16 on page 2 of this Guide)

W43.5 £

total boxes W43.1 to W43.5

W43.6 £

box W43.6 x 15%

W43 £

Notional tax *is not repayable and so has to be calculated as an allowance given in terms of tax rather than being regarded as tax deducted at source.*

- **Partnership notional tax** (from box 4.78)

W44.1 £

+

- **Notional tax on UK scrip dividends and FIDs** (from boxes 10.22, 10.25, 10.28 and 10.31)

W44.2 £

+

- **Notional tax on estate income** (from box 7.14)

W44.3 £

total boxes W44.1 to W44.3

W44 £

- **Tax credit relief on foreign income and treaty relief on UK income** (and see the notes on page 9 of this Guide)

from boxes 6.9 and 9.35

W45 £

boxes W41 to W45

W46 £

box W39 *minus* box W46

W47 £

Income Tax due, after allowances and reliefs
If the figure in box W46 is more than the figure in box W39, enter a zero

- **Recoverable tax on charitable covenants, annuities, Gift Aid and Millennium Gift Aid payments** (box W17 x 23%)

W48 £

- **Class 4 National Insurance Contributions** (from box 3.91 or box 4.25)

W49 £

boxes W47 + W48 + W49

W50 £

Income Tax and Class 4 National Insurance Contributions

Copy the figure in box W50 to box W50 on page 8

Tax Calculation Working Sheet

Calculating your tax bill - continued

▶ *(copy figure from box W50 on page 7)* **Income Tax and Class 4 NIC due** W50 £

- *Unpaid tax for earlier years included in PAYE code for 1998-99* W51 £

Copy the figure in box W51 to box 18.1 in your Tax Return

box W50 + box W51 W52 £

Tax paid at source

- *Employment* (from boxes 1.11 and 1.30) W53.1 £
- *Self-employment* (from boxes 3.92 and 3.120) W53.2 £
- *Partnerships* (from box 4.77) W53.3 £
- *UK land and property* (from box 5.21) W53.4 £
- *Foreign income* (from boxes 6.1 and 6.3) W53.5 £
- *Trusts, settlements or estate income* (from boxes 7.2, 7.5, 7.8 and 7.11) W53.6 £
- *UK savings* (from boxes 10.3, 10.6, 10.10, 10.13, 10.16 and 10.19) W53.7 £
- *UK pensions, retirement annuities and benefits* (from boxes 11.8 and 11.11) W53.8 £
- *Other income* (from box 13.2) W53.9 £

total boxes W53.1 to W53.9 W53 £

- *Tax due for 1998-99 included in 1999-2000 PAYE tax code* W54 £

Copy the figure in box W54 to box 18.2 in your Tax Return

box W53 + box W54 W55 £

Total tax and Class 4 NIC due for 1998-99 (overpayment in brackets) W56 £

box W52 minus box W55

Copy the figure in box W56 to box 18.3 in your Tax Return

Tax owed or overpaid in 1998-99

- *1998-99 tax already refunded* (from box 17.1) W57A £
- *Tax due for earlier years* W57 £

Copy the figure in box W57 to box 18.4 in your Tax Return

boxes W56 + W57A + W57 W58 £

- *Tax overpaid for earlier years* W59 £

Tick box 18.5 and copy the figure in box W59 to the 'Additional information' box on page 8 of your Tax Return

- *Payments already made* (from your Statements of Account) W60 £

box W59 + box W60 W61 £

Tax you owe for 1998-99 W62 £

box W58 minus box W61

OR

Tax you have overpaid for 1998-99 W63 £

box W61 minus box W58

Payments on account for 1999-2000

If there is a figure in box W62, add it to any figure in box W59. If the total is less than £1,000 and you would like the amount you owe collected through your 2000-2001 tax code, copy W62 to W64. Otherwise enter zero W64 £

box W56 minus box W64

If W65 is less than £500, you do not need to make payments on account. Leave box 18.6 blank and tick box 18.8. If W65 is equal to or more than £500, carry on W65 £

- *Income Tax due, after allowances and reliefs* W66 £

from boxes W44 + W47 + W48

- *Class 4 National Insurance Contributions* W67 £

from box W49

box W66 + box W67 W68 £

box W68 x 20% W69 £

If W65 is less than W69, you do not need to make payments on account. Leave box 18.6 blank and tick box 18.8. If W65 is equal to or more than W69, you do have to make payments on account. Fill in box W70

This is the amount of each payment on account for 1999-2000 W70 £

box W65 x 50%

Copy the figure in box W70 (including pence) to box 18.6 in your Tax Return

Reference Notes

Pension Schemes' data _____

_____

Mortgage data _____

_____

Company car detail and other benefits _____

_____

_____

Investment notes _____

_____

PEP details _____

_____

TESSA details _____

_____

ISA details _____

_____

Dividends, interest, etc. _____

_____

_____

_____

_____

_____

_____

_____

Reference Notes

Private health scheme details_____

_____

Payroll giving schemes and gift aid amounts_____

_____

Deeds of covenant_____

_____

_____

_____

Expenses notes _____

_____

_____

_____

Insurance matters (check values each year) _____

_____

_____

Home and contents ☐ Personal belongings ☐ Life ☐ Accident, etc. ☐

General reminders_____

_____

_____

_____

_____

_____

_____

Personal Reminders

National Insurance Number ....

Tax Reference Number ....

Tax Office Address ....

....

....

Tax Returns	Date sent to tax office	Date agreed with Inland Revenue
1997	....	....
1998	....	....
1999	....	....

	1997–98	1998–99	1999–2000
PAYE Code Checked	☐	☐	☐
P60 Form from employer checked	☐	☐	☐

Notes on correspondence:

....

....

....

....

....

....

....

....

....

REMEMBER:

With self assessment tax legislation the law requires you to keep all records of earnings, income, benefits, profits, expenses, etc. and all other relevant information for 22 months from the end of the tax year if you are employed, and for 5 years and 10 months if you are self-employed.

Rates of tax and allowances

Income tax	1999–2000	1998–99	1997–98
Lower rate at 10%	£1,500	-	-
Lower rate at 20%	-	£4,300	£4,100
Basic rate at 23%†	£1,501–£28,000	£4,301–£27,100	£4,101–£26,100
Higher rate at 40%	over £28,000	over £27,100	over £26,100

Income tax is payable on your total income, earned and unearned, after deducting your personal allowances and allowable expenses.

†The 20% rate instead of basic rate applies to savings income.

Capital gains tax			
The rate for individuals is the same as their income tax rate.			
Exemption limit	£7,100	£6,800	£6,500

Inheritance tax			
Rate 40% –			
Exemption limit	£231,000	£223,000	£215,000

VAT rate	17.5%	*17.5%	*17.5%
VAT registration			
turnover level	£51,000	£50,000	£49,000
	from 1.4.99	from 1.4.98	from 1.12.97
VAT deregistration			
turnover level	£49,000	£48,000	£47,000
	from 1.4.99	from 1.4.98	from 1.12.97

*8% on domestic fuel, reducing to 5% from 1.9.97.

Corporation tax – Full rate 31% from 1 April 1997; 30% from 1 April 1999. Small companies rate 21% from 1 April 1997; 20% from 1 April 1999

Personal allowance	£4,335	£4,195	£4,045
Married Couple's allowance	††£1,970	†£1,900	†£1,830

Age allowance			
Aged 65–74 personal	£5,720	£5,410	£5,220
married couple's	††£5,125	†£3,305	†£3,185
Aged 75 & over personal	£5,980	£5,600	£5,400
married couple's	††£5,195	†£3,345	†£3,225
but there are income restrictions			
Income limit	£16,800	£16,200	£15,600

Additional personal allowance	††£1,970	†£1,900	†£1,830
Widow's bereavement	††£1,970	†£1,900	†£1,830
Blind person's allowance	£1,380	£1,330	£1,280

†relief restricted to 15 per cent   ††relief restricted to 10 per cent

Tax Organiser and Diary

1999 TAX RETURN
2000 TAX RETURN

SIGNIFICANT DATES

Make first payment on account if applicable (see page 29) **31 JAN 1999**	Make first payment on account if applicable (see page 29) **31 JAN 2000**
You should receive a 1999 tax return **APRIL 1999**	You should receive a 2000 tax return **APRIL 2000**
Request any supplementary pages from tax office (ring 0645 000404) (fax 0645 000604) **APRIL/MAY 1999**	Request any supplementary pages from tax office (ring 0645 000404) (fax 0645 000604) **APRIL/MAY 2000**
Make second payment on account if applicable **31 JULY 1999**	Make second payment on account if applicable **31 JULY 2000**
Send in completed tax return **30 SEPT 1999**	Send in completed tax return **30 SEPT 2000**
Send in tax return if you want to calculate your own tax and pay any 1998-99 balance **31 JAN 2000**	Send in tax return if you want to calculate your own tax and pay any 1999-2000 balance **31 JAN 2001**

When you fill in the new self-assessment tax return, you only have to put *total* figures in the various boxes. Use the following work sheets to record your figures.

Use the left-hand columns in the following work sheets to keep a record of how you arrived at these figures, not only as a convenient means of adding them up but also in case the tax office asks for the details.

Use the right-hand columns in the following work sheets to keep an ongoing record throughout this next year as a reminder of significant figures or events during 1999–2000 so that when you get next year's tax return to complete you have the information at your fingertips.

What you entered in your 1998–99 tax return

Reminders to help you fill in your 1999–2000 tax return

INCOME FROM INTEREST & DIVIDENDS

Paperwork to keep: Interest statements, dividend vouchers, National Savings Certificates.

Interest received and tax deducted

Interest received and tax deducted

Are your investments in joint names? – see page 9

Are your investments in joint names? – see page 9

What you entered in your 1998–99 tax return

National Savings

_____

_____

_____

_____

_____

_____

_____

_____

_____

Dividends and tax deducted

_____

_____

_____

_____

_____

_____

_____

_____

_____

Reminders to help you fill in your 1999–2000 tax return

National Savings

_____

_____

_____

_____

_____

_____

_____

_____

_____

Dividends and tax deducted

_____

_____

_____

_____

_____

_____

_____

_____

_____

If most of your income is from investments you may be due a refund – see page 11

**What you entered in your
1998–99 tax return**

**Reminders to help you fill in your
1999–2000 tax return**

INCOME FROM U.K. PENSIONS, RETIREMENT ANNUITIES & SOCIAL SECURITY BENEFITS

Paperwork to keep: State pension book or details; P60 form for other pensions; DSS statements

State pension details

State pension details

**Other pensions and annuities
and tax deducted**

**Other pensions and annuities
and tax deducted**

Social Security benefits

Social Security benefits

OTHER INCOME

Paperwork to keep: Receipts and statements for casual earnings and expenses claimed

Other income

Other income

Expenses claimed

Expenses to be claimed

Remember to claim
expenses – see page 34

Remember to claim
expenses – see page 34

What you entered in your 1998–99 tax return

Reminders to help you fill in your 1999–2000 tax return

PAYMENTS ALLOWED FOR TAX

Paperwork to keep:Pension statements; interest certificates; covenants; Receipts for expenses, etc

Payments to pension schemes, etc.

Top up your pension contributions before the tax year ends – see page 16

Payments to pension schemes, etc.

Top up your pension contributions before the tax year ends – see page 16

Expenses claimed (vocational training, subscriptions, loan interest, maintenance, etc.)

Take advantage of mortgage interest allocations – see page 18

Expenses claimed (vocational training, subscriptions, loan interest, maintenance, etc.)

Take advantage of mortgage interest allocations – see page 18

Charitable giving (covenants, gift aid, etc.)

Charitable giving (covenants, gift aid, etc.)

It might be beneficial – see pages 23 & 25

It might be beneficial – see pages 23 & 25

PERSONAL ALLOWANCES

Do you need to consider transferring unused allowances to your wife or husband? ❑

Do you need to consider transferring unused allowances to your wife or husband? ❑

What you entered in your 1998–99 tax return

Reminders to help you fill in your 1999–2000 tax return

EMPLOYMENT

Paperwork to keep: P60, P45 & P11D forms, receipts for benefits, invoices for expenses, etc.

Diary note:

P60 due from employer by   31 MAY 1999
P11D due from employer by   6 JULY 1999
Check your PAYE code   FEB/MAR 1999

Diary note:

P60 due from employer by   31 MAY 2000
P11D due from employer by   6 JULY 2000
Check your PAYE code   FEB/MAR 2000

Changes in employment (dates, etc.)

Changes in employment (dates, etc.)

Car mileage log

Getting close to 18,000 business miles near the year end? – see page 61

Car mileage log

Getting close to 18,000 business miles near the year end? – see page 61

Car changes (details)

Car changes (details)

Benefits received from employer

Benefits received from employer

Expenses claimed

Check what's available – see page 34

Expenses to be claimed

Check what's available – see page 34

**What you entered in your
1998–99 tax return**

**Reminders to help you fill in your
1999–2000 tax return**

SHARE OPTIONS

Paperwork to keep: Share option certificates, correspondence from trustees, market valuations

Share options granted, exercised, etc.

Share options granted, exercised, etc.

SELF EMPLOYMENT & PARTNERSHIPS

Paperwork to keep: All account books, sales and purchase invoices.

Diary check

VAT limit OK? ❏   NI Payments OK? ❏

Payment on account made _____

Accounts completed ❏

Other notes:

Diary check

VAT limit OK? ❏   NI Payments OK? ❏

Payment on account scheduled _____

Accounts preparation ❏

Other notes:

There will be interest charges if you are late with 'on account' payments – see page 29

There will be interest charges if you are late with 'on account' payments – see page 29

**What you entered in your
1998–99 tax return**

**Reminders to help you fill in your
1999–2000 tax return**

INCOME FROM LAND & PROPERTY

Paperwork to keep: Records of rents received; records of expenses and bills for them.

Rent-a-Room Scheme

Rent-a-Room Scheme

Rent income received

Rent income received

Expenses claimed

Expenses to be claimed

Check expenses on page 46

Check expenses on page 46

FOREIGN INCOME & EXPENSES

Paperwork to keep: Overseas dividend vouchers, details of pensions, foreign tax assessments, etc

Income and tax paid

Income and tax paid

Expenses claimed

Expenses to be claimed

What you entered in your 1998–99 tax return

Reminders to help you fill in your 1999–2000 tax return

INCOME FROM TRUSTS, SETTLEMENTS, ESTATES etc

Paperwork to keep: Dividend and interest vouchers; Form R185E, Trust correspondence

Interest

Interest

Dividends

Dividends

Other notes

Other notes

CAPITAL GAINS

Paperwork to keep: Contract notes for sale or purchase of shares; Invoices and letters for sale or purchase of other assets; Invoices for allowable expenses.

Assets purchased

Assets purchased

Assets sold

Assets sold

Expenses claimed

Expenses to be claimed

Indexation/tapering relief note

Indexation/tapering relief note

Losses brought forward or carried forward

Losses brought forward or carried forward